COACHED BY JESUS

31 LIFE-CHANGING QUESTIONS ASKED BY THE MASTER

ALAN NELSON

OUR PURPOSE AT HOWARD PUBLISHING IS TO:

- *Increase* faith in the hearts of growing Christians
- *Inspire* holiness in the lives of believers
- *Instill* hope in the hearts of struggling people everywhere

BECAUSE HE'S COMING AGAIN!

Published by Howard Publishing Co., Inc.
3117 North Seventh Street, West Monroe, Louisiana 71291-2227
www.howardpublishing.com

05 06 07 08 09 10 11 12 13 14   10 9 8 7 6 5 4 3 2 1

Edited by Heather Gemmen
Interior design by John Mark Luke Designs
Cover design by Kirk DouPonce

Library of Congress Cataloging-in-Publication Data

Nelson, Alan E.
Coached by Jesus : 31 life changing questions asked by the Master / Alan Nelson.
p. cm.
ISBN 978-1-4516-2378-9
1. Christian life. 2. Jesus Christ—Example. 3. Personal coaching. I. Title.

BV4501.3.N443 2005
248.4—dc22

2005050284

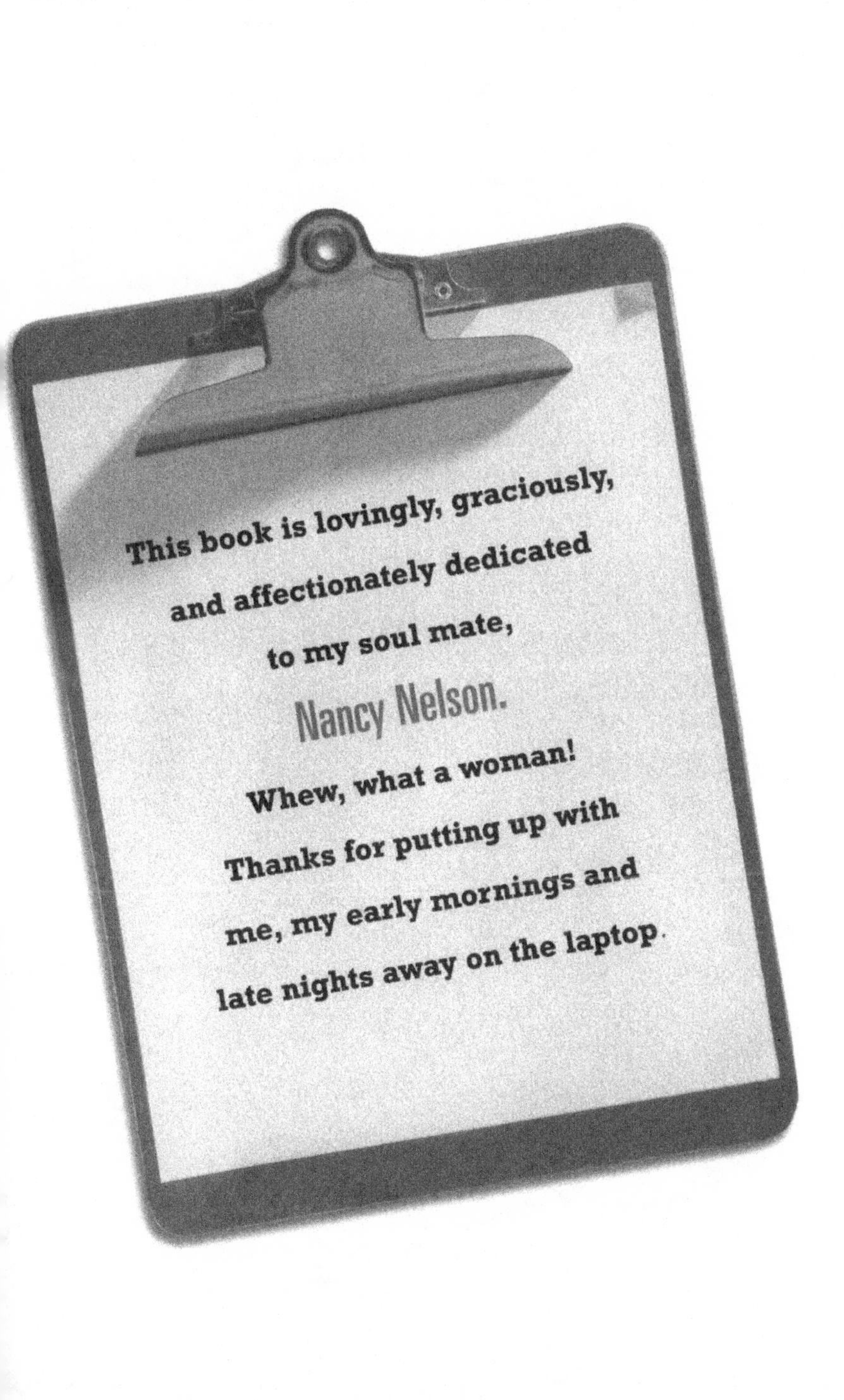
This book is lovingly, graciously,
and affectionately dedicated
to my soul mate,
Nancy Nelson.
Whew, what a woman!
Thanks for putting up with
me, my early mornings and
late nights away on the laptop.

CONTENTS

CONTENTS

ACKNOWLEDGMENTS

Special thanks to Denny and Philis Boultinghouse, Heather Gemmen, and the team at Howard Publishing for believing in these ideas.

Thanks also to readers Alicia Barker, Ranie Cahill, Kathi Carbonaro, and Diana Hunt.

INTRODUCTION

You have the potential for greatness. You have what it takes to make a difference in the world. With the right coach helping you unleash your slumbering possibilities, nothing—no one—can stop you. As the player who allows the coach to shape him into a star quarterback, you can allow Someone to teach you to achieve greatness by using what you already possess.

In this age of heightened competition and complexity, traditional education does not always produce the desired results. It's time that we rediscover the ancient practice of coaching: cultivating seeds of greatness by asking strategic questions—questions that cause us to think new thoughts and make new connections. Many of the great philosophers and teachers—like Socrates, Aristotle, and Jesus—used strategic questions to teach their students and mature their disciples.

Of all the great teachers throughout history, most believe that Jesus was the greatest. But if you were asked to name even one of the strategic questions that Jesus asked, could you do it? This book gives you the opportunity to contemplate not one, but thirty-one of these potent questions as recorded in the New Testament gospels—questions that still have pertinence today. These enduring, ageless insights have the ability to catalyze new growth in you so that you can experience the spiritual yet practical effect of the Master's wisdom.

Imagine for a moment what it would be like to be coached by the greatest Teacher who ever lived. Jesus's teachings have profoundly changed the lives of millions throughout history. What if we looked at His influence through the lens of coaching? What if we focused on the questions that Jesus asked people who desired to understand the deeper dimensions of their potential? *Coached by Jesus* is a tool to help you experience history's greatest Teacher in personal and meaningful ways.

Originally, the word *coach* referred to a means of transporting a person from one location to another (e.g., most of us who travel fly "coach"). The modern use of the term, in the context of human development, conveys inner travel, whereby a person moves from one place to another by responding to probing questions and taking action steps. This movement results in growth, transporting you toward the person you are meant to become.

A targeted question directs our attention to strategic growth areas. It has a way of engaging us, empowering us. An insightful question increases the chances of application, as we tend to own our own answers more than someone else's. A question can be less demeaning than a lecture, for it encourages us to think on our own. It doesn't assume we're ignorant or lack answers. Vital questions enhance our thinking skills.

As a leader and spiritual coach (pastor), I personally have seen over the last two decades the power that comes from mixing coaching with spiritual growth and renewal. Coaching is exceptionally productive among adult learners, and with that in mind I have designed this book to provide daily coaching sessions with Jesus. As you move through these thirty-one coaching sessions, you will find that as Jesus poses His questions, He doesn't dictate, but rather challenges you to engage in the process of thinking. He never forces you to believe a certain way, but He prompts you to discern what is important through the power of strategically asked questions.

As you prepare to begin your journey through these coaching sessions, choose a quiet, uninterrupted time and place. Focus your attention on these questions; ponder them deeply. Let them sink into your mind and spirit, then write or speak your responses to Him. You may choose to study one question each day for a month, or you may prefer to consider each session for a week. The sessions have a similar format: Each is titled with a *paraphrased question* posed by Jesus in one of the New Testament gospels. Following this title is the *actual verse* the question is taken from.

During each session we'll look at the question asked by Jesus and massage the idea a bit to see what *application* it might have in your life. The goal of this book is not to teach the more obvious lessons typically deduced from these historical passages. Rather, the aim is to uncover fresh perspectives from familiar passages.

Next the Let's Get Personal section takes you just a bit deeper, with three or four questions that help you search your self and where you are in your journey.

Each session ends with Let's Get Going, a set of questions designed to help you *reflect* and *act* on the coaching session. Reflection without action is an intellectual endeavor yielding little growth; action without reflection tends toward busyness and creates habits that benefit little.

Rather than reading through this book in one sitting, use the sessions as your daily workout. The energy comes in working through one section at a time and letting it strengthen your mind and soul. Some sessions will likely have more personal relevance than others. This is to be expected. Consider using this book in an accountability group. Growth pursued together can be more enjoyable and effective than individual study.

Ingesting these questions and exploring the truths of the Master's teaching will enable you to authentically claim, "I've been *Coached by Jesus*." I commend you for taking this vital step toward realizing your potential. Jesus is ready to be your life coach.

SESSION

ARE YOU MAKING A DIFFERENCE?

You are the salt of the earth. But if the salt loses its saltiness, how can it be made salty again?

—MATTHEW 5:13

The right amount of salt enhances the flavor of food without drawing attention to itself. A dash of this simple white ingredient awakens an entrée's dormant flavors. But Jesus's question isn't about salt; it's about you: How are you improving the conditions around you? Are you making a difference? Are you looking for ways to help others more than you are looking for ways others can help you? Are you seeking ways to enhance the beauty around you?

Salt has a distinct flavor, and so do you. Out of millions of possibilities, God formed you. Of the billions of people who have and will ever breathe the air of this earth, you are the one God chose to live in your skin. You are unique. Even identical twins have different fingerprints. As genetic coding is unraveled and cloning becomes an approaching reality, remember that no one can copy your individuality. There are times when only your hug will dry a tear of someone close. Your grin can salve the chaotic emotions of a harassed store clerk. Your compliment can inspire a child not to give up. Knowing that your calling is unlike others', consider how you will leave your mark on the people around you.

KNOWING THAT YOUR CALLING IS UNLIKE OTHERS', CONSIDER HOW YOU WILL LEAVE YOUR MARK ON THE PEOPLE AROUND YOU.

Bland people are users—consumers who absorb the gifts, time, and resources of others. They ultimately take more out of the world than they give. Self-centered people are as common as potatoes. You can be the one to stand out, to spice things up. But keep in mind that salt doesn't steal the show from food; it simply highlights the existing flavor. Likewise, you can add value to the world around you. Let your behavior cause the waitress to say, "I'm glad he sat in my area." Strive to make your boss boast, "I'm the one who hired her." Live life in a way that enables your friends and family to say, "We're so lucky to have you in our lives." Subtly, quietly, make a difference in everything you do and everywhere you go.

Jesus is talking about your unparalleled role in life, but He puts an interesting twist on it. He asks, how can salt, having lost its saltiness, regain its flavor? How do we lose our saltiness? Do we lose it by forgetting our uniqueness, by allowing the machinery of society to squeeze us into its mold as it conditions us to think that we're just like everyone else? In this question, is Jesus calling you to use the gifts He has given you?

You're free to be you. Your true individuality is fulfilled when you enhance the lives of others. You serve best when you help others in the areas of your strengths. Discover your particular qualities. Explore the possibilities. Experiment to uncover what you're good at. Don't beat yourself up by comparing the strengths of others with your weaknesses. Don't elevate yourself by contrasting your abilities with others' inabilities. Know your strengths and use them—to serve others and thus fulfill yourself.

When you ponder your saltiness, don't limit your flavor to career dreams or large life accomplishments. Salt is a common ingredient that can make a big difference. We often overestimate the impact of a few, large contributions and underestimate the value of many small ones. In the living of each day are opportunities for you to leave a positive mark on the planet. Recognize and seize them. You have a calling from your Creator to live a salty lifestyle, using your one-of-a-kind influence and embracing opportunities to make a difference. Don't lose your flavor.

LET'S GET PERSONAL

Jesus always knew just what buttons to push in those He taught in order to help them take a long, hard look at their hearts. The question we're examining today could be expanded into three new ones to help us do just that:

- Where are you the most salty? In other words, where do you make the biggest difference in life?
- How have you accented the lives of others in small, common, "salty" ways?
- How do you enhance others' lives, rather than drawing attention to yourself?

Vigilance is required to maintain your saltiness. The busyness of life has a way of leeching the God-given saltiness out of you. Don't let this happen. Fight for it. Don't let others intimidate you or corrupt your desire to leave your mark, to make a difference. Consider each day an opportunity to enhance the flavor of the lives of those around you. You have only one shot on earth to find your flavor and release it. Are you making a difference?

LET'S GET GOING

1. Write down three of your strengths.
2. What tempts you to give up being salty?
3. How can you increase or regain your saltiness?

SESSION

2

WHY DO YOU WORRY?

Therefore I tell you, do not worry about your life, what you will eat or drink; or about your body, what you will wear. Is not life more important than food, and the body more important than clothes? Look at the birds of the air; they do not sow or reap or store away in barns, and yet your heavenly Father feeds them. Are you not much more valuable than they? Who of you by worrying can add a single hour to his life?

And why do you worry about clothes? . . . If that is how God clothes the grass of the field, which is here today and tomorrow is thrown into the fire, will he not much more clothe you, O you of little faith?

—MATTHEW 6:25–28, 30

Jesus is not just preaching generic truths to a crowd of strangers in His famous speech commonly referred to as the

Sermon on the Mount; He is talking to His closest friends. These people had given up their jobs in hopes of doing something more important with their lives. In the back of their minds they're stressed about the basics—things that all of us think about, *How am I going to pay the bills? What if I don't have enough money to feed the kids? How am I going to keep my family clothed?*

Jesus's disciples did not have a monopoly on worry. For most of us, fretting about food, wardrobes, and everyday basics comes naturally. We don't have to go to school to learn how to worry. Anxiety may be Americans' favorite pastime. Relaxant medications are the most prescribed drugs. Bars are populated with stressed-out people who are self-medicating at the conclusion of anxious days. When we have difficulty accepting life as it is, we often pursue relief, no matter how artificial or temporary. We voluntarily induce our anxieties by stewing over unworthy matters, believing that our fretting is productive.

Some people mistakenly suggest that Jesus was saying that things such as food, clothes, and work are unimportant. What He was telling them is that worrying is not productive and that attention should be paid to more vital matters. When you weigh the amount of daily energy that is consumed by pursuing things as basic as food and clothes, you begin to realize how much of that focus could be invested in more important things such as people, God, work, ministry, and personal growth. Jesus would encourage us to turn our energy toward more productive action, to invest it where it will have an eternal impact.

Worry is actually low-grade fear: we're afraid of losing what we value. Tug on your worry string, and it will lead to what you value—health, security, food, clothing, money, or love. When you think you may lose or fail to obtain what is valuable to you, fear is a natural response. For example, you may panic when you reach into your pocket and realize that your wallet is missing. You wouldn't have that reaction if you didn't value the wallet. When you put your trash out by the curb on garbage day, you do not lose sleep worrying that someone will take it; you don't care because it's of no value to you.

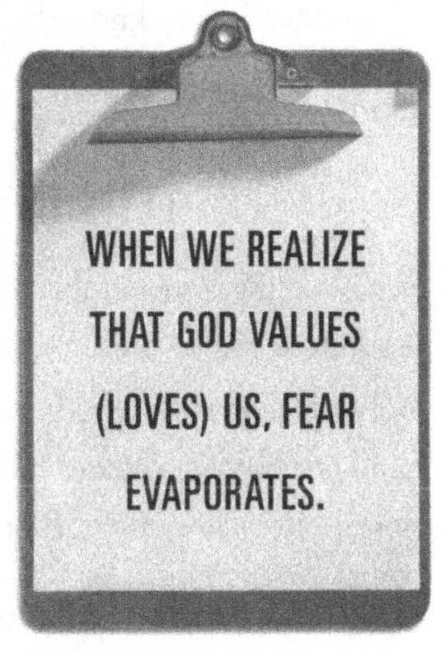
WHEN WE REALIZE THAT GOD VALUES (LOVES) US, FEAR EVAPORATES.

Jesus's question shines a spotlight on how much God loves and values us. When we realize that God values (loves) us, fear evaporates. We gain new confidence in living, and our anxiety disappears. People may not like what we wear, our bank account may not afford us the material accouterment that we desire; but none of these matters need affect us significantly, because the overwhelming truth is that we're loved by the Creator of the universe.

In Jesus's question, "Why do you worry?" He calls us to rise above the petty concerns of this world and replace them with His stability and peace. He wants us to live abundantly. The words of the well-known Serenity Prayer point us to the God who is able to grant the peace we crave:

> God grant me the serenity
> to accept the things I cannot change;
> courage to change the things I can;
> and wisdom to know the difference.
> —Reinhold Niebuhr

LET'S GET PERSONAL

Not worrying does not mean being irresponsible. Jesus simply reminds us that it is God who controls the details of our lives and that God cares deeply for us. With that in mind we can hand our burdens over to Him. Jesus asks three specific questions to help determine what you value:

- What do you worry about?
- What benefit does your worrying provide?
- How might your concerns reflect what you value?

Worry undermines our self-esteem. It gives us a sense of being out of control, a feeling that we have little impact on cause and effect and that we're victims-in-waiting. The truth is that we don't have control over much in our lives. Fretting over things that are outside of our control or are insignificant is a waste of valuable energy.

You're not the god of your micro-universe, but the good news is that the Creator of the macro-universe cares for you. We don't have to be careless, but we do need to care less.

Why do you worry? Can God be trusted to provide for your needs? Can you then invest your energies in what matters more?

LET'S GET GOING

1. Write down the top three things you worry about.
2. How do your worries reflect your values?
3. Are the values you listed above enduring values, or can you think of more significant matters?

SESSION

3

WHAT ARE YOUR BLIND SPOTS?

Why do you look at the speck of sawdust in your brother's eye and pay no attention to the plank in your own eye? How can you say to your brother, "Let me take the speck out of your eye," when all the time there is a plank in your own eye?

—MATTHEW 7:3–4

You know what it's like: someone wearing too much bling condemns the neighbor for owning a Lexus; a woman calls you up to complain about how much her friend gossips; a child tells a parent that his brother tattles all the time. Even as you're reading this, you're probably thinking of someone else who notices others' faults rather than his or her own. This question gives us a keen insight into the realm of personal growth. When we're tempted to examine what's wrong in another person, it's a reminder to ponder our own failures and to investigate potential blind spots in our own lives. It's always easier to notice the black speck stuck in someone else's teeth than to spot the green lettuce marring our own smiles. That's human nature.

It may be tempting to critique those who criticize, to shame those who fail to apply the truth Jesus is teaching. But God has not appointed us to speck-pick at speck-pickers! Resist the temptation to become exasperated with those who do not "get it." If you "get it," if you harness this truth, you'll be amply rewarded by humbly working on yourself.

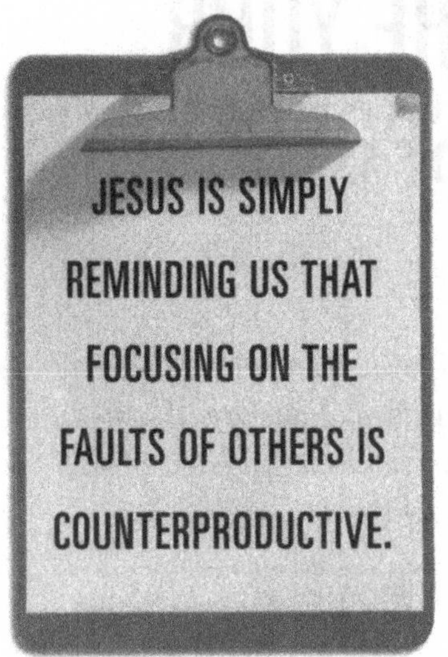
JESUS IS SIMPLY
REMINDING US THAT
FOCUSING ON THE
FAULTS OF OTHERS IS
COUNTERPRODUCTIVE.

"But what about others?" you may ask. "Who's going to correct those plank-laden, speck-picking people in my life?" The lesson may very well come from you, but not by poking at their planks. You'll do it by quietly modeling a Christ-centered life, confessing your own failures in appropriate moments, and whispering responses such as, "I've struggled with that myself from time to time," or, "We all have our weak points, don't we?"

Jesus is not suggesting that we never point out other

people's weaknesses—especially if they are harming themselves or others. He's simply reminding us that focusing on the faults of others is counterproductive. Other people's weaknesses can be left to God to handle.

Our view of others is often not so much one of factual observation as much as subjective perspective. Anais Nin wrote, "We see things not as they are, but as we are." Realize that when we hear people talking about someone else in less than positive terms, we're often learning more about the person talking than the person being talked about. We tend to find what we're looking for. If you're seeking the negative in others, you'll always find something to confirm your theories. If you're striving to uncover the best in others, you'll likely find verifications. When you catch yourself focusing on the errors and omissions of others, ask yourself why you're even looking for weak spots. What are your motives for pointing out the negative in others? Your answer will tell you something about yourself.

Jesus was never blind to the pluses and minuses of others. He was a master at reading both actions and motives. But when you observe His approach with people, you see that the only ones He consistently confronted with the error of their ways were the professional speck-pickers, those individuals whose habitual condemnation prevented them from seeing the planks in their own eyes.

Sometimes we're prone to notice the flaws in others that

mirror our own. We recognize them because we're familiar with them. At other times we spot the weaknesses in others that are in contrast to our strengths. We don't understand why they cannot do the things that come so easily to us.

Another kind of criticism is caused by forgetting our pasts. Our tolerance often wanes for those who struggle with what we've conquered. (The most critical nonsmoker is a former smoker.) Our victory in one area can become a failure in the arena of grace and patience with others.

Or it may be that we may pick on others to divert attention from ourselves. By keeping the spotlight on others' deficiencies, we hope to keep those around us distracted from noticing our weak points and to avoid facing our own need for personal growth.

We all have blind spots—areas in our lives where we fail or are vulnerable—that we do not see. They wouldn't really be blind spots if we were aware of them. To assume you don't have weaknesses is ignorance; to insist you don't have them is arrogance. Once you uncover your blind spots, the temptation to critique others will remind you to work on your own frailties and to extend more grace toward others.

LET'S GET PERSONAL

A blind spot, in this context, is not literally caused by a physical barrier. Jesus is asking three questions regarding the temptation to critique others and to try to change them by pointing out their weaknesses.

- Are you interested in detecting your own weaknesses?
- What might be your potential blind spots?
- What do you learn about yourself when you notice the failures of others?

Today's coaching session teaches us to use our natural inclination to notice the weaknesses in others as a means of self-awareness and improvement. Are you ready to face yourself?

LET'S GET GOING

1. How might your irritation about others' weak points serve as a diversion from working on yourself?
2. What are three things about yourself that you want to improve? How can the awareness of these keep you humble and gracious when dealing with others?
3. Who could you approach to get honest feedback about your blind spots?

SESSION

WHO CAN YOU TRUST?

"Which of you, if his son asks for bread, will give him a stone? Or if he asks for a fish, will give him a snake? If you, then, though you are evil, know how to give good gifts to your children, how much more will your Father in heaven give good gifts to those who ask him! So in everything, do to others what you would have them do to you, for this sums up the Law and the Prophets."

—MATTHEW 7:9–12

Trust is the currency of relationships, but you can't trust everyone. They don't deserve it. Whom to trust and to what degree are vitally important matters. But Jesus is not just concerned about this as a social issue for you; it is a spiritual matter. Faith and trust are fraternal twins. You have faith in what you trust, and you trust what you have faith in.

Sometimes people naively say things such as, "I'm not a person of faith." All of us demonstrate faith every day without blinking an eye. We drive our cars at outrageous speeds in the opposite direction of strangers doing the same; we do not know these people and can't be sure they'll stay on their side of a skinny yellow line, but we don't hesitate to be on the road. We sit down to eat food prepared for us by complete strangers, trusting that they're not trying to poison us and that the health codes are adequately maintained. We drop off our kids at school, having faith that the teachers and administrators will care for our loved ones in our absence.

The illustration Jesus uses to describe trust is the relationship between a parent and child, perhaps the most revered bond in life. Our civil laws are strict toward parents who betray this sacred trust, and society is deeply troubled when people who care for children on a parent's behalf (such as baby-sitters, teachers, and clergy) prove undependable. Perhaps this is because we all know that our early relationships condition how we trust or distrust others. Our pasts affect our future faith. Everyone is wired differently and responds to betrayal in various ways, but trust is essential in order to experience a healthy or intimate relationship.

Sometimes people don't trust others because they themselves are not trustworthy. Trust is a bridge that allows people to connect. When trust is firmly established, other valuables such as love, encouragement, constructive criticism, empathy, and humor can be safely conveyed. But when the bridge is broken, these precious commodities are withheld, and the people on both sides of the bridge find that their souls are starving.

After calling people to consider the issue of trust, Jesus offers a piece of wisdom that has become known as the Golden Rule: "Do to others what you would have them do to you." This is a proactive, rather than a reactive, principle. Do you show up when you say you'll be there? Do you keep a confidence when information is shared with you? Do you follow through on a task for which you're responsible? The prevailing rule in Jesus's day, and of course the norm today, erodes trust: "Do to others what they do to you." When people behave poorly toward you, the natural tendency is to respond in-kind. However, the Golden Rule calls us to rise above the norm. In doing what is right, you significantly increase the chances of being treated well because most people operate from the old rule of responding in-kind. By initiating

TRUST IS A BRIDGE
THAT ALLOWS PEOPLE
TO CONNECT.

a positive action, you create trust. When others reveal their untrustworthiness, take note; but don't let that change who you are.

The bigger lesson here, of course, is one of trusting God. Your perception of God determines how you trust Him. If your God view is less than positive, consider why. Your view of God influences the way you see life and respond to challenges. These are very significant matters that probe the depth of our trust levels and determine whether or not we try to live life in our own capabilities.

God is good. He gives good gifts. Do you believe that? Or do you sense He might give you a stone if you asked for a piece of bread? When we do not see God as trustworthy, we're not apt to pray. We may or may not be active in church life, depending on what we get out of it socially or whether we feel obliged by conditioning. But when it comes to our one-on-one relationship with our Creator, our lack of trust in Him shows up in how we "do life." When you operate in your own strength, with little dependence on His guidance, it's a sign that you feel God is untrustworthy. Think about what has tainted your view of God.

Toxic thoughts of God litter the lives of good people—people who want more from life but doubt that God is a keeper of promises. We may have collected this impression from bad experiences with influential people in our pasts. We might suffer from spiritual ignorance, simply a lack of understanding about God and Jesus. Some people have distorted God thoughts based on a toxic-church experience or failed leader, both of which have little to do with God Himself.

LET'S GET PERSONAL

It is unlikely that Jesus was responding to a specific situation of a father's giving his son a bad gift. He was simply making the point that if earthly fathers can be trustworthy, then the Father in heaven, who is love, will do what is right for you. Jesus's coaching allows us to look at trust from three angles.

- Whom do you trust?
- Are you trustworthy?
- Why do you or do you not trust God?

Jesus's coaching session today reaches deep into our souls, yet affects our daily life: whether or not we return a phone call, rely on a friend, or pause to pray for God's intervention. Trust is a very precious commodity in life, so work hard at building a wealth of it. What is your current condition? How do others see you? Are those closest to you trustworthy? If not, do you need to invest in some new friends? Do you need to make amends or extend forgiveness? God calls on you to trust in His inherent goodness and giving nature. Do you?

SESSION 4

LET'S GET GOING

1. On a scale of 1 to 5 (1 = low; 5 = high), how would you rate yourself in terms of being trustworthy?
2. On a scale of 1 to 5, how would you rate the trustworthiness of those closest to you?
3. On a scale of 1 to 5, what level would you rate your faith (trust) in God?
4. What can you do to improve these ratings?

SESSION

5

WHAT DO YOU HAVE?

His disciples answered, "But where in this remote place can anyone get enough bread to feed them?"
"How many loaves do you have?" Jesus asked.
"Seven," they replied.

—MARK 8:4–5

What a dilemma! Over five thousand men, plus women, teens, and children, had converged on the side of a hill to hear Jesus speak. "What's the dilemma?" you ask. What preacher or teacher wouldn't enjoy a large, enthusiastic audience? The problem is that there were no—shall we say—facilities. Sure, the trees and rock piles probably doubled as au naturel rest rooms, but how do you feed this many people who had remained longer than anticipated, enamored by Jesus's teachings?

Jesus questioned the disciples about feeding the crowd, but supplies were woefully short. They had studied the situation, gathered a few loaves, and logically deduced, "It can't be done."

While the disciples were focusing on what they didn't have, Jesus taught them a powerful lesson with a single question, "How many loaves do you have?" Every trip begins from the starting point—the place where you are. Pilots file flight plans that designate departures and intended destinations. You can't really plan a journey until you've carefully assessed where you are now. "What do you have?"

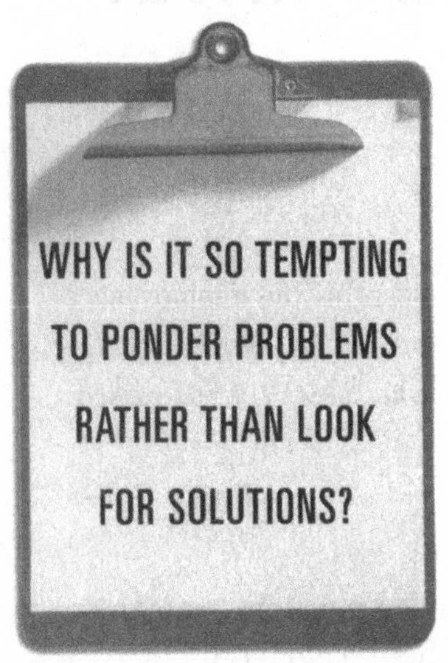
WHY IS IT SO TEMPTING
TO PONDER PROBLEMS
RATHER THAN LOOK
FOR SOLUTIONS?

Why is it so tempting to ponder problems rather than look for solutions? We look at what others have, where others are, and then proceed to focus on what we don't have and where we're not. The running joke about men and their remote controls is that women are interested in what's on TV while men are interested in what *else* is on TV. We observe this same truth in other situations: A pastor visits a renowned church and says, "I don't have the heritage of that pastor," or "I didn't wind up in such a growth-ripe community." The woman attending a cocktail party thinks, *If I only had that woman's husband, I'd be a lot happier.* A businessman calling on a successful client ponders, *I don't have the education or network that this guy has. If I did, I'd be occupying this corner office with a view.* The inner-city social worker thinks, *We can't do much with our limited resources. The suburbs have all the finances, talent, and resources. It's not fair.*

You get the picture. Our perceived lack keeps our attention on the problem and off the solution. We rationalize it as a legitimate desire to find a remedy, but by turning our attention toward what we don't have, we may be striving to legitimize our desire to give up. "What's the use? We're underfunded, overtaxed, and faced with an unconquerable situation. Raise the white flag. Everyone will understand." We slowly limp off the playing field, convinced that it just "wasn't in the cards" for us to do better. Maybe the disciples were reporting on the lack of available food and resources so they could in essence throw up their hands and say, "There's nothing much we can do. I guess we'll have to send everyone home and set up camp for the night. At least we tried, but our responsibility is over. It's been a long day."

The work is never complete until we've taken an assessment of what resources are available and then exhausted those possibilities. Jesus's question calls us to focus on available supplies (possible solutions) as opposed to unavailable ones (obvious problems). The other lesson He teaches is that miracles occur only when circumstantial outcomes are humanly unobtainable. We're most primed for a miracle, an act of God in our lives, when we perceive no objective solution—like Moses with his back to the Red Sea, David facing Goliath, Joshua surrounding Jericho, or even Jesus attending the wedding reception that ran out of wine. The situation need not be life-or-death, feast-or-famine. Consider the little, everyday circumstances when you're tempted to give up, quit, or justify defeat by focusing on what you lack.

Sometimes the assessment of what you have doesn't say you can't accomplish a feat; it only determines the means by which you'll experience victory. By realizing they didn't have sufficient food, the disciples assumed they couldn't feed the crowds. Jesus knew it would require unconventional means to solve the problem.

LET'S GET PERSONAL

Do you think Jesus didn't know how many loaves of bread were available? Or do you think the answer would have affected what He did next? No. Jesus asked this question for the sake of His followers, not for Himself. He was really asking:

- What do you have to offer?
- Do you expect God to use your gifts to perform a miracle?
- Do you see solutions or problems?

Regardless of your situation in life and the assets of others, your attention needs to be on where you are and what you have. This is where miracles can grow. Do you assume that what others have is what they always had? Do you ever compare your starting points with other people's destinations? Your lot in life is to use what you have, to make it available to God, and then to chart your unique path. Look at what you have, not at what you don't, and then surrender those resources into the hands of the Master. What's in your lunch bag?

LET'S GET GOING

1. Describe a present goal you have that seems overwhelming and that you're inadequately prepared to face.

2. What do you now have that can help you move toward that goal?

3. Why do you focus on what you don't have?

SESSION

HOW FRESH IS YOUR FAITH?

He said to them, "If any of you has a sheep and it falls into a pit on the Sabbath, will you not take hold of it and lift it out? . . . And why do you break the command of God for the sake of your tradition?"

—MATTHEW 12:11; 15:3

Some people confuse religion with faith. Jesus never claimed to be a religious leader. In fact, in this coaching session Jesus clarifies the difference between spiritual growth and church activity. Don't get me wrong: Jesus was not against organized worship. He visited and taught in the temple. He created everything in life to have some sense of organization—whether the cycle of seasons, the human body, or even grapevines. But He knew to focus on essence, differentiating package from contents, style from significance, medium from message, symbolism from meaning, performance from purpose, means from ends.

Tradition is the repetition of a worthwhile practice, whereas *traditionalism* is paying homage to a practice devoid of its original purpose. The romantic notion we give to religious activities is often little more than emotional conditioning, like a favorite song while dating evokes memories years later, the sight of an old friend elicits fond thoughts of the past, and smells resurrect the feelings of previous experiences. When people go to church to feel good (or to look good), they lose the meaning behind the activity. The religious zealots of Jesus's day elevated the value of the Sabbath, the dedicated day of worship, above the act of helping others, a higher priority. Jesus was not advocating that they ignore a day of God worship, but He was pointing out the very subtle line between worshiping God and the traditions of God worship. Spiritual growth and worship must take forms, but human nature often confuses a package with its contents.

Earlier, when Jesus's followers had asked Him to teach them how to pray, He told them not to pray as the pagans do, with meaningless chatter. He then gave them a model prayer, commonly known as the Lord's Prayer. "Our Father who art in heaven . . ." Most avid churchgoers can rattle off this prayer like a child chants a nursery rhyme, barely engaging the brain, rarely the emotions. Ironically, we allow a prayer given as an antidote to meaningless babble to become just that. Reciting prayers and scriptures by rote while disengaging your mind and heart from spiritual activities does little to mature you.

Some people look at the meaningless religious traditions of others and allow them to interfere with their own spiritual growth. "I'm not going to be like one of those hypocrites. They piously go to church but don't really know God. All organized religion is bogus." Letting someone else's worship of a religious tradition turn you off to soul growth is a weak excuse for failing to develop your own vibrant relationship with God. The reverence for having no traditions is as detrimental as placing overemphasis on traditions.

LET'S GET PERSONAL

Jesus's words implore us to consider how our religion gets in the way of our spiritual growth. Here's what He's asking you:

- How might your practice of religious traditions hinder authentic, deeper spiritual growth?
- Is religion or faith more important to you?
- Are you more concerned with looking good or doing what is right?

We often respond to God, not as He is, but as we think He is. A false mental image of God is as bad as a false metal image—an idol. While many people proudly boast of their spiritual prowess, Jesus was advocating a different approach to knowing God: humble authenticity. You must work hard not to let a callus grow on your soul after repetitive acts of worship. Keep worship fresh. Let God surprise you from time to time. Intentionally tear up your boxes containing your tamed deity. Traditions are often little more than divine bridles, making us think we can rein in the supernatural as we desire. Even good habits can lose their benefit, as grooves that keep us on track become ruts that prevent us from growing.

In today's coaching session Jesus is prompting you to consider how your worship traditions may be hampering your relationship with Him. Practices have the tendency to become stale, cold, and external. God yearns for our warm hearts. He longs for an organic, renewed approach to Him. Fight the temptation to confuse external actions with internal travel. How fresh is your faith right now?

LET'S GET GOING

1. How have your religious experiences benefited or thwarted your spiritual growth? (Sometimes they can do both.)

2. What religious activities should you decrease or stop due to lack of vibrancy?

3. What can you do to freshen up your relationship with God?

SESSION

7

WHAT CAN YOU GIVE IN EXCHANGE FOR YOUR SOUL?

What good will it be for a man if he gains the whole world, yet forfeits his soul? Or what can a man give in exchange for his soul?

—Matthew 16:26

Jesus coaches us today with what may be the ultimate life question. He originally used it as He was sharing some startling news with His followers: He would be leaving. No one likes to hear bad news. We often respond to it with denial, anger, numbness, and argument. But amidst this announced interruption to their previously scheduled plans, Jesus invited them to ponder something more deeply. What is it they want to gain from their short lives here on earth? He asks the same thing of you today.

Everyone has goals in life, even if they are merely to survive, find food and work, and obtain basics for the family. Most of us are blessed to have dreams, higher aspirations for meaning and purpose. These motivate us. They consume our time, energy, talent, and financial resources. Jesus asks you to consider what turns your crank, what gets you out of bed in the morning. Think about your dreams and aspirations. Ponder your motivation.

Some people are disconnected from their inner drives. Can you articulate your dreams? Do certain topics engage your interest when discussed? Do specific things excite, frustrate, and make you glad or sad? These are likely the themes of your life that determine where you'll put most of your energy. Examine your ambitions against the eternal time line to determine whether they're temporary and will disappear with a downturn in the market or will rust if it rains.

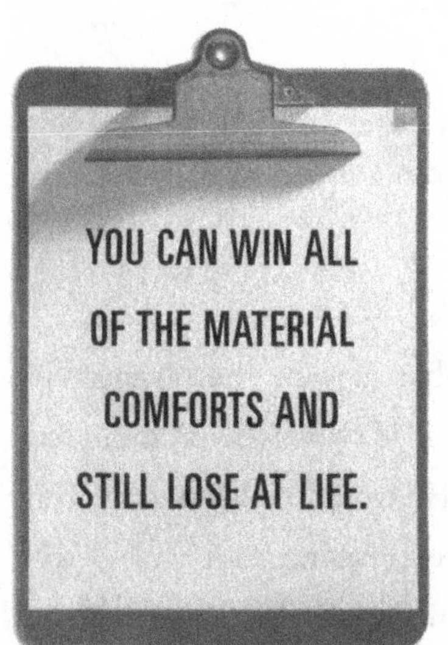
YOU CAN WIN ALL
OF THE MATERIAL
COMFORTS AND
STILL LOSE AT LIFE.

Sometimes people misperceive Jesus, thinking Him to be antiachievement, akin to some passive cave dweller, avoiding the realities of life. On the contrary, Jesus is very pro-achievement. But all accomplishments are not created equal.

Some deteriorate and blow away like a discarded burger wrapper. Others have the ability to extend into eternity. Jesus's concern is about what you're pursuing in life. He realizes that the herd effect, following what others do, influences us toward pursuing material goods and possessions. Look around you. A large part of our culture dreams of bigger homes, nicer cars, deeper bank accounts, and looking like we've "made it." The problem is that you can win all of these material comforts and still lose at life. Jesus challenges you to pursue loftier goals, higher ambitions. Raise the bar.

We all have soul holes, places in our inner beings that yearn to be filled. These include a spiritual connection with our Creator, our relationships with people, and a purpose that incorporates our passions and talents. If these holes are not filled with meaningful resources, we resort to artificial substitutes, such as looks, physical possessions, and status. If these are not obtainable in satisfying quantities (and they rarely are), we move toward anesthetizing our pain with pleasurable stimulants: illicit sex, drugs, alcohol, and adrenaline-inducing experiences. These activities are little more than self-medications, as we strive to deaden the pain of our empty soul holes. Many, many people fall for these trivial pursuits.

The culmination of these approaches is summed up by Solomon who wrote: "Utterly meaningless! Everything is meaningless. What does a man gain from all his labor at which he toils under the sun?" (Ecclesiastes 1:2–3).

Soul-hole fillers include four primary issues:

- Who you are as a person: character development and spiritual and emotional maturity.
- Who you are in your connection with God: knowing Jesus, growing spiritually.
- Who you are in your relationships: loving, forgiving, encouraging, serving.
- Who you are in your higher purpose: using your time and talents uniquely.

These are to be the focal points of any person's life; sadly, most people invest a majority of their time and energy in vain pursuits. If you're going to focus on these four elements, you'll need to march to the beat of a different drummer, eliminating the superficial and concentrating on what Coach Jesus is emphasizing.

LET'S GET PERSONAL

I hope you know that Jesus's question is rhetorical. He is not asking you to seriously consider what you would exchange for your soul. What He is asking you to consider is this:

- What motivates you most in life, and how do you know this?

- Does your ambition have an eternal nature, or is it temporary?
- What can you do to fill your soul holes God's way?

Today's coaching session asks deeply probing questions about what motivates your actions. Jesus is challenging you to see what most do not, to look beyond the common goals in life and to pursue what matters most. Think in terms of the eternal. Everything else goes away after you leave earth. You can't take anything with you, but you can send certain treasures ahead. What motivates you, and is it worthwhile?

LET'S GET GOING

1. List your four primary ambitions in life. Now look at your calendar and bank account, and determine how your ambitions are or are not being supported by your time/money expenditures.
2. Which people around you seem to be motivated by things that are temporary? How can you avoid taking their path?
3. What might change in your daily schedule and lifestyle if you seriously strive to implement today's coaching session?

SESSION

8

WHEN DO YOU MOVE ON?

> *"O unbelieving and perverse generation,"* Jesus replied, *"how long shall I stay with you? How long shall I put up with you?"*
>
> —MATTHEW 17:17

The coaching session today has to do with the duration of your relationships. Wisdom is required to know when a connection with another person should continue and when it should end. Undoubtedly, most people give up too soon in relationships when they seem burdensome and irritating, whether it is with a spouse, employee, best friend, boss, or neighbor. When we fail to persevere, we retard character growth. Spending time with difficult people exercises our tolerance and exposes our deficiencies. We discover that we need to work on patience, people skills, and forgiveness.

People who quickly move from relationship to relationship do little more than pick up their baggage and move down the road. They sweep the dust under the rug. They sever ties with those who know them too well so they won't have to face their weaknesses. They convince themselves that everyone else—not the person in the mirror—has all the problems. Jesus was an advocate of forgiving those who offend. He said to forgive seventy times seven times—meaning until we've lost count. Our most common problem is giving up on people when there is much to be salvaged from relationships.

Yet there come times when the wisest decision is to pull up stakes, cut ties, and move past a relationship. After you've done all you can to persevere and the person ceases to be helped by your presence, it may be time for a change. Endless patience is not necessarily grace. It may be dysfunction. Codependency occurs in a relationship between a person who only lives to care for a person in need and someone who takes the assistance without any intent to change the situation. Would it be healthy for you to ask, "How long should I stay with this person?"

Are you a caretaker? Keep in mind that abusive people who are unwilling to budge in their behavior seldom change. They have worth as individuals, of course, but the bigger issue is why you feel the need to continue in an abusive relationship. God never takes away a person's freedom of choice. When people habitually decide to use their free will for destructive purposes, you can't change them. Believing you can is to consider oneself more powerful than God. It is either delusion or pride, neither of which is realistic.

What you need in such a situation is divine wisdom—ask God. Some misunderstand the idea of unconditional love. Love has conditions; it always has, and it always will. You are called to love, not to be a mercy zombie. At times, only by withdrawing conventional love can we hope to jar a person free from his own self-destruction. By bailing out a person with an incessant drive toward injury and pain, we actually enable him. Even our presence creates a reward system that subconsciously says, "Your attitudes and actions are not that bad. I'll stick around whether or not you change."

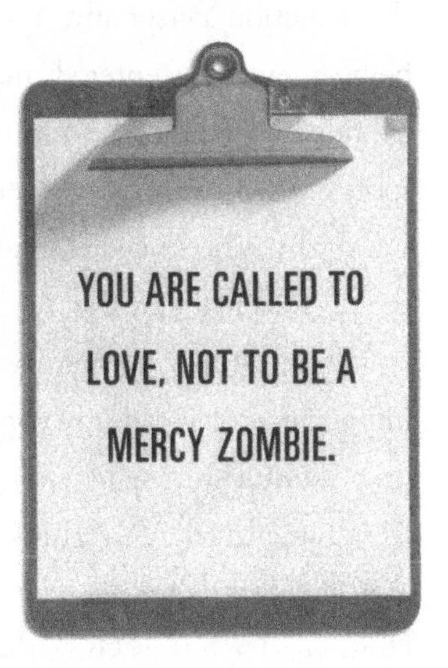
YOU ARE CALLED TO
LOVE, NOT TO BE A
MERCY ZOMBIE.

When a person persists in self-destructive or others-destructive behaviors and has been confronted, a nonrepentant person may need to be let go. In the famous parable of the prodigal son, the father waits for his son, but he doesn't go out searching for him. He readily forgives and calls for a party when the son returns home, but Dad was strong enough not to go after him. Counselors realize that only those who want to be helped can be helped. Good counselors do not chase after clients; they do not give away advice; they establish healthy boundaries.

Have you been a recipient of another person's decision to draw the line in your relationship? It is difficult not to take the rejection personally. You may feel the other person is being unfair, self-centered, and impatient. It could be that you do not understand the futility of your ways, because blind spots conceal the truth. Over time you may come to understand why others needed to pull back from you and recognize the need to make necessary changes in your life.

Those of us who believe in people and understand the importance of getting beyond ourselves may see giving up on a relationship as irresponsible. Jesus constantly coaches us to hang in there, to think more of others than ourselves, and to express grace and forgiveness to those around us. However, He lets us know there are lines that, if crossed, require us to responsibly withdraw our commitment to others. He wants us to expend our energy on those who will receive our love.

LET'S GET PERSONAL

Was Jesus grumbling about His miserable assignment of hanging out with foolish people? It sure sounds like it. But we know that God is love and that Jesus's heart was deeply concerned for His people; He walked away from people only after they had rejected Him. We can emulate His behavior by asking these questions:

- How long should I endure?
- Is it time to give up on a relationship?
- Am I willing to suspend a dysfunctional relationship?

In today's coaching session we learn that there is a season to be patient with people and a season to give up on dead-end relationships. You are not God. The power of free will means that we are at times unable to influence them for good. When a person decides to take a path of self-destruction, we may not be able to exert any influence. We need wisdom to know how long we should endure with him or her. Evaluate your current relationships to determine which deserve endurance and which need to be discontinued.

LET'S GET GOING

1. How do you know how long to endure with a person?
2. Is there anyone in your life with whom you have probably endured long enough?
3. What are the pros and cons of giving up on a specific difficult relationship?

SESSION

WHEN DO YOU FIGHT?

Then Jesus told his disciples a parable to show them that they should always pray and not give up. . . . "There was a judge who neither feared God nor cared about men. And there was a widow . . . who kept coming to him with the plea, 'Grant me justice against my adversary.'

"For some time he refused. But finally he said to himself, 'Even though I don't fear God or care about men, yet because this widow keeps bothering me, I will see that she gets justice, so that she won't eventually wear me out with her coming!'"

And the Lord said, . . . "Will not God bring about justice for his chosen ones, who cry out to him day and night? Will he keep putting them off? I tell you, he will see that they get justice, and quickly."

—LUKE 18:1–8

Sometimes you can't reach a goal, can't get someone to respond to your needs, can't accomplish what you've set out to do. Been there. Done that. Human nature yearns for gratification. Our rapid-fire society conditions us to want it fast—instant is best. When the microwave seems slow, traffic lights take an eternity, your computer seems out of date within a year, or you feel at a loss without a cell phone, chances are you're at risk. Being vulnerable in the endurance department will cause you to experience far less than you'd like in life.

In addition to the need-for-speed weakness, we've become a hopelessly disposable-crazy society, at least in the westernized areas of the world. Look at the size of our garbage cans and landfills—or even the amount of refuse at the end of a fast-food eating experience. We toss our old phones, computers, and clothing. Customer loyalty is a thing of the past. It is survival of the fittest; we'll take whoever responds best to our whims and needs, and we hardly try to discern between the two. In our culture we dump jobs, marriages, and even babies if they fail to satisfy us or if they threaten to cramp our styles. "You only go around once in life," we declare, as we expediently cut the ties that bind us.

In today's coaching session Jesus is teaching us a lesson that may have more application today than it did in the time that He gave it. Life was difficult yet simpler in those days. People were more apt to be patient and to persevere because things moved more slowly. But the lesson of perseverance has more to do with faith than it does our existing culture. It's a human-nature quirk that is exacerbated when times tempt us to give up too quickly. Which knock on the door did the unjust judge answer? Was it the last one or an accumulation of all of them? If the woman had quit knocking, she would not have received a response.

HUMAN NATURE USUALLY GIVES UP TOO SOON ON THINGS THAT MATTER.

Human nature usually gives up too soon on things that matter. We set a goal, and when we run into a snag, we go a different direction or give up altogether. But certain things—often the most important and fulfilling ones—can be achieved only through perseverance. Making a baby is easier than raising a child. Falling in love and getting married is rather simple; staying hitched is quite another matter.

Think about what you're tempted to give up on. Consider how the gauge would read, if your attitude and actions were monitored by a faith detector. Have you regretted anything you have given up on in the past? Don't repeat your mistakes. List how things might have turned out if you had persevered. It's not so much a matter of guilt and remorse but of learning from the past. If you're always moving on, you'll rarely move forward.

Notice that in Jesus's story, we never find out whether or not the woman won her case. What she was looking for was an attempt at justice. Perseverance isn't some magic wand to get whatever it is we want from life. But if we are to have any hope of obtaining our goals, we'd better learn the importance of not giving up. Perseverance and faith are two sides of the same coin.

Faith is primarily attitudinal in nature, having to do with the relationship of one thing with another. The attitude of a plane refers to its relationship with the horizon. The attitude of a person has to do with the way he or she approaches circumstances. An attitude of faith means that a person faces a situation with hope. The belief is that the desire or wish will eventually come to fruition. Perseverance is a natural expression of faith. When we give up trying, we lack faith.

Persevering is not passive waiting. The woman in Jesus's story persisted in banging on the unjust judge's door. She didn't knock once and leave, waiting for him to "get in touch with her at his convenience." When Jesus referred to waiting, it was an active process, not a static one disengaged from activity. "Not taking no for an answer" can be annoying; it can also reflect perseverance. The person being nagged sees it as harassment, but the person who is enduring sees it as determination.

LET'S GET PERSONAL

Jesus is not trying to turn us all into nags; He is encouraging us to be tenacious fighters of justice. He asks:

- Are you putting anything off, confusing waiting with persevering?
- What have you emotionally given up on that is still within your grasp?
- What door do you need to knock on again and again, until you get a response?

Sometimes the wisest decision is to pull the plug, admit defeat, and move on. But the greatest error in life is giving up too soon, becoming a victim of circumstances, and whining your way through life. Snap out of it. Grit your teeth. Don't quit. You've got the Wisdom of the universe on your side. While perseverance doesn't always pay off, giving up rarely does. What's worth fighting for right now where you're tempted to quit?

LET'S GET GOING

1. What are some things in your life for which you're fighting?
2. What is making perseverance difficult for you?
3. What attitude or value do you need to adjust so that you don't justify giving up prematurely?

SESSION

10

HOW GOOD ARE YOU?

"Why do you call me good?" Jesus asked him. "Only God is truly good."

—LUKE 18:19 NLT

Surveys show that the average person thinks he or she is above average. Regardless of looks, IQ, character, ability, or work ethic, most people rank themselves higher than others. This is what might be referred to as unreliable optimism. While some suggest that this response is little more than good self-esteem, today's coaching session presents a counterintuitive look at ego issues. Psychology has taught us much about our identity, the ego, the "I." Self-image is how we perceive ourselves.

Are there benefits to humility, to not thinking you are more significant than others? Of course. First of all, you're better at serving others. It's difficult to serve well when you feel that you're stooping to help them. When pride creates arthritis in your joints, kneeling and bowing become painful experiences. An inability to serve limits your work, ministry, friendships, and family life. Thus, a benefit of humility is better relationships.

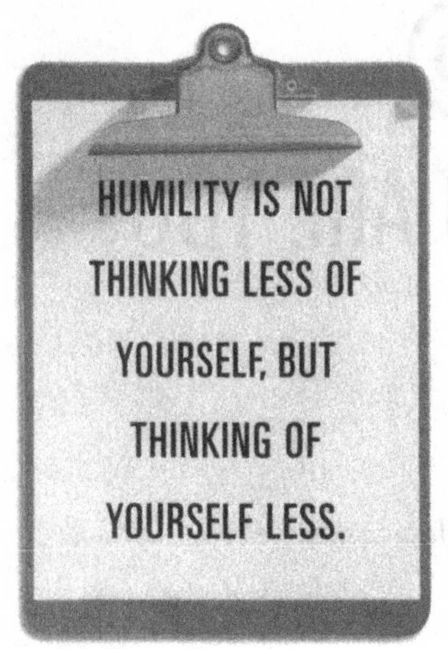
HUMILITY IS NOT
THINKING LESS OF
YOURSELF, BUT
THINKING OF
YOURSELF LESS.

Secondly, you're easier to be around. Humble people are low maintenance. They tend to shy away from high-maintenance types. Friendships and working relationships feel more fulfilling with humble folk. The flip side of being more easily liked is that humility makes it more difficult for others to offend you. Pride is easily offended and, as a result, causes significant irritation. A benefit of humility is less stress.

Another benefit of humility is personal growth. Humble people possess a teachable attitude. They do not claim to already know the answers, thus reducing what they need to unlearn. Change is more difficult for those who are smug with their knowledge and experience. *Humility* and *humus* are from the same root meanings. Humility is fertilizer for the soul, the sort of spiritual dirt that grows character fruit well. Not claiming to be an authority keeps you teachable.

Pride distorts the dependability of our advice. We appear to be better than we really are. But eventually, people discover that we overestimate our skill and knowledge. They make conscious adjustments to compensate for our inflated opinions, downsizing us, sometimes appropriately, but sometimes too far. Better to promise less and oversupply than to promise much and disappoint. A secret of customer satisfaction is to exceed expectations. Studies show that a person who seems less perfect on a résumé is more apt to be hired, because employers assume the applicant is being truthful and thus more reliable.

Dismissing a compliment has downsides. You run the risk of offending the person. And people may perceive you as feigning humility instead of being truly humble; fake piety is considered gratuitous and irritating. Humility is not thinking less of yourself, but thinking of yourself less. Pride, on the other hand, tends to think more of oneself as well as thinking of oneself more. Do not succumb to the myth that suggests you must be proud to get ahead in life, to promote yourself and to race with the fastest. Elitism is epidemic. Stand out among the rest—be genuinely humble.

The dilemma most of us face is ego imbalance. We tilt toward feeling above average and begin to believe our own press releases, feeling in some way that we're better than others and that, for whatever reason (looks, education, age, experience, wealth, ethnicity, morality, or spirituality) others don't meet our standards. Go too far in the other direction and you diminish the inherent value that God has placed in you. The resulting lack of confidence disables you from helping others as you should. Keeping your ego in balance is the challenge.

LET'S GET PERSONAL

A man approached Jesus with a question and addressed Him as "Good Teacher." Before responding to the man's question, Jesus took a brief time-out to resist the title. "Why do you call me good?" He asked. In defense of the well-mannered inquisitor, we might follow up with a counterquestion of our own. Why would Jesus ask this? Did He suffer from low self-esteem? Why would He have a problem being referred to in such a complimentary fashion? While Jesus does not directly reject the compliment, He deflects it, keeping it from sinking in. Instead, He takes the humble approach that focuses attention on God rather than absorbing it Himself.

- What do you do to intentionally cultivate humility in your life?
- What can you do to emulate the sort of attitude that authentically refuses to think of yourself as better than others?
- What are the signs of stealth pride that sneaks into our lives?

Jesus is modeling how we can kindly deflect others' attempts at putting us on a pedestal. Jesus's dismissal of the compliment was not because He didn't deserve it, but because He was more concerned for the man's soul than His own recognition. Humility is a character trait that is to be applauded as much as any life quality, but the Teflon nature of it refuses to let compliments stick. How good do you think you are?

LET'S GET GOING

1. How would you rate yourself on pride? (1 = very humble; 5 = very proud)
2. Who is someone in your circle who emulates confident humility? Why does having a model of humility help in pursuing this trait?
3. Have you found any "tricks," tactics, or favorite phrases for accepting compliments without absorbing them?

SESSION

HOW MUCH ARE YOU WILLING TO PAY?

Then the mother of Zebedee's sons came to Jesus with her sons and, kneeling down, asked a favor of him.

"What is it you want?" he asked.

She said, "Grant that one of these two sons of mine may sit at your right and the other at your left in your kingdom."

"You don't know what you are asking," Jesus said to them. "Can you drink the cup I am going to drink?"

—Matthew 20:20–22

The mother of two of Jesus's twelve closest followers approached Him. Each had more than likely given up full-time employment, a good amount of family life, and even a reputation in order to follow Jesus. Mom, looking out for her two boys, wanted to make sure they were well compensated. She thought she'd help them a bit by going to Jesus and securing His commitment. Perhaps they'd talked about it over dinner. Maybe the two sons had put her up to it. More than likely, she was merely being a dedicated mother. Unfortunately, Jesus's response wasn't what she was hoping for. You'd think that for all the brothers had given up, Jesus would have been more obliging.

In the culture of Jesus's time, a groom would negotiate with the father of the bride a dowry, a price to replace the loss of his daughter in the family. When the amount was suitable, the father would pour a cup of wine and offer it to the groom for him to drink, sealing the deal. "Drinking the cup" meant agreeing to pay the price.

We all want things in life, whether it's finding a mate, landing a good job, losing weight, running a marathon, or being respected. Focusing on the end result is understandable, but counting the cost and committing to the price require more determination.

Pursuing rewards without sacrifice works against us. Billions of dollars are spent in gambling every year. People hope for something significant for little or no effort. The few, well-publicized winners and the manipulative method of random-reward psychology compel well-meaning people to give away their lives, lining the pockets of tempters rather than investing. There is a positive correlation between paying the price and enjoying the reward. Trophies that are passed out, regardless of performance, are never valued as much as those that cost the participant sweat, effort, and risk.

Accomplishment without cost not only diminishes our enjoyment, it also renders us no character development. Having power and resources without adequate character is dangerous. A person who is grounded prior to obtaining success is like a house with a strong foundation. When we try to avoid paying the price, our ability to both acquire and retain our reward is undermined. History is full of stories about people who received what cost them little, causing them to tilt out of balance. Struggle adds ballast to our lives. It lowers our emotional and spiritual center of gravity so that we can stand up under stress.

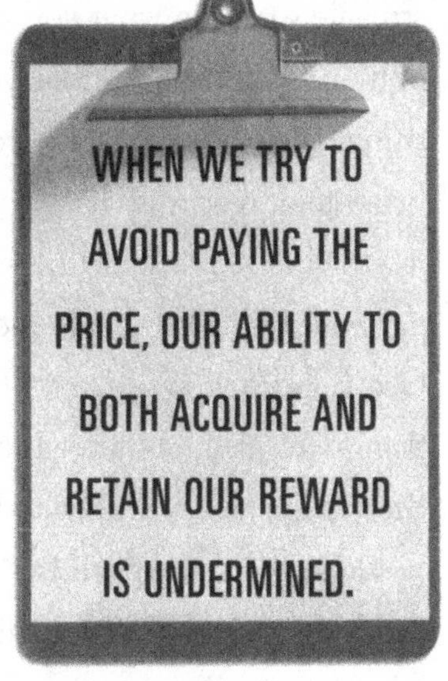
WHEN WE TRY TO
AVOID PAYING THE
PRICE, OUR ABILITY TO
BOTH ACQUIRE AND
RETAIN OUR REWARD
IS UNDERMINED.

Consider both the costs and the potential rewards of anything you desire to achieve. Focusing on one without the other is unrealistic. If you only look at the price tag without the benefits, you'll never achieve much because you'll be discouraged before you begin. When you weigh only the benefits without the cost, you become overwhelmed when the inevitable difficulties arise. Finish lines are nearly always more difficult to reach than we imagined. Success at all costs is a bad investment. If the ratio is too great, the joy of achievement will be diminished.

You want a good marriage? It's going to cost you. Don't jump into "I do" until you've pondered the price. Quit complaining about your lot in life as though you deserve a handout or acting as if you'd be better off if you didn't have to struggle to attain what you want. Why are you above others? Why do you suppose that you'd be better off getting something for free? What makes you think that you'd not be ruined by a life of reward that cost you little or nothing? Everything worthwhile costs someone something. If you're unwilling to pay your bill, who should pick up the tab? Why should they? Get smart. Grow up. Face reality. Deal with it. The best things in life are not easily obtained. This doesn't mean they're not worth it, but rather that they won't be cheap or hassle free. Giving birth is a painful, risky process, but the rewards are astounding. Obtaining a degree from a reputable school is challenging, but the process pays off. Getting up early to exercise is not fun, but the discipline of the task yields fruit.

Even after this discussion, you'd think there might be some sort of formula that says if you work hard, you'll always get good results. The disciples' mother was not only asking Jesus for a certain position for her sons' sacrifice; she was also implying that she'd like a guarantee. She wanted to make sure that after all they were risking, they'd be certain to have places of power and importance. Jesus did not give that. You can work hard and still not obtain what you desire. Pursuing accomplishments does not guarantee success, but thinking you can achieve them without cost is almost a guarantee you'll achieve nothing.

LET'S GET PERSONAL

Jesus knew exactly what the mother of these men wanted. Why would He ask such an obvious question? He wanted to provoke growth in her, and He wants to do the same for us. He asks:

- What is it you want to achieve?
- Do you really "know what you are asking"?
- Are you willing to pay the price to get what you want?

In today's coaching session Jesus is helping us confront the normal, natural inclination to want something for nothing. Have you found the precarious, healthy balance between hope that inspires and realism, which helps you stay motivated? What is it that you want in your life? Can you and will you pay the price for what you desire?

SESSION 11

LET'S GET GOING

1. Make a list of what you want to accomplish.
2. What are the benefits/rewards you're hoping for by pursuing these goals?
3. What are the realistic costs and potential risks inherent in these goals? Can you "drink the cup"?

SESSION

WHAT DO YOU WANT?

As Jesus approached Jericho, a blind man was sitting by the roadside begging. When he heard the crowd going by, he asked what was happening. They told him, "Jesus of Nazareth is passing by."

He called out, "Jesus, Son of David, have mercy on me!"

Those who led the way rebuked him and told him to be quiet, but he shouted all the more, "Son of David, have mercy on me!"

Jesus stopped and ordered the man to be brought to him. When he came near, Jesus asked him, "What do you want me to do for you?"

—LUKE 18:35–41

Well-trained receptionists ask qualifying questions that we would do well to repeat dozens of times each day, "How may

I help you?" "What do you want from me?" "Specifically how can I serve you?" Effective communication is difficult. People frequently send mixed messages. Often they don't really know what they are seeking from us. No matter what we do, we're liable to miss the mark. The result is often criticism, disappointment, strained relations, and wasted energy. We create unnecessary stress when we fail to clarify the needs and wants of others as well as our own expectations of them.

If Jesus understood the blind man's request, why would He ask this question? One reason might have been to ensure the success of their interaction. When we engage others, we enter into an informal contract with them, which will hopefully be mutually beneficial. By asking others to state their wishes, we reduce confusion and increase the likelihood of fulfilling our unspoken obligation to help them. For example, if we're selling clothes and the customer says he's looking for brown slacks, we can avoid other colors; this saves time and energy for both parties and lets us know when we've fulfilled our part of the tacit agreement. By asking people to state their desires, we increase the chances of meeting their expectations.

A lack of clarity creates unnecessary tension in relationships. Incorrect assumptions often result in mutual frustration. Unmet expectations are the greatest stresses in relationships and often occur because of poor communication. Respect a relationship enough to ask the questions. Value your time and effort sufficiently to ask the questions.

By avoiding assumptions you also determine whether or not you are able or willing to serve the other person. On one occasion a man came to Jesus, asking Him to resolve an inheritance dispute he was having with a family member. Unwilling to get involved in the matter, Jesus declined to mediate, deciding rather to use the situation as a teachable moment to talk about greed. When we fail to clarify, we often get involved in situations that we later regret, either because we're ill equipped to respond or we lack motivation to complete the request. Sometimes we say yes and other times no too quickly, because we don't take the time to seek definition, thus regretting decisions or missing greater opportunities.

Marriage is a state where the clarity question comes up frequently. A wife may be disappointed because she did not clearly express her desires to her husband. She gets lazy about communicating her expectations, thus setting up her mate to fail.

A husband may assume his wife can read his mind. He may get angry at her failure to understand, when in reality it was his lack of clarity that caused the problem.

LET'S GET PERSONAL

"What do you want me to do for you?" What kind of question is that? Everyone could see what he wanted. The man couldn't see. He was blind. What else would a blind man want than to be healed? Perhaps Jesus was testing him, making sure he had faith. Jesus's modeling is an effective coaching session for us, because the need for expectation clarification is an important life lesson. Jesus is asking us three things:

- Do you clearly articulate your expectations of others?
- Do you seek clarification from people before trying to serve them?
- What can you do to improve the way you go about discerning the expectations of others?

Making assumptions is an irresponsible and sometimes dangerous way to handle your relationships, whether personal or business. It's also a root of reduced productivity, hurt feelings, and wasted energy. When someone requests your help, seek clarification. You want to do what you can to serve that person in the best way possible.

LET'S GET GOING

1. Can you think of a recent example where expectations were not met in a relationship?
2. How could clarity have been improved beforehand?
3. What is one thing you can do to clarify a current situation in your life?

SESSION

13

WILL YOU GET THE JOB DONE?

"What do you think? There was a man who had two sons. He went to the first and said, 'Son, go and work today in the vineyard.'

"'I will not,' he answered, but later he changed his mind and went.

"Then the father went to the other son and said the same thing. He answered, 'I will, sir,' but he did not go.

"Which of the two did what his father wanted?"

—Matthew 21:28–31

Jesus was talking to a group of religious folks who seemed to have a lot of spiritual answers, but whose lives did not reflect genuine spiritual character. They were gold-painted, silver-plated, but not solid bullion. Jesus tells a story about a man with two sons. When asked, one son said he'd work in the vineyard, but didn't follow through. The other son did not commit initially, but ended up working as his father asked. The obedient son was the one who actually worked, because the father was not as interested in hearing the answer he wanted as much as seeing the action he expected. While these religious people appeared to be close to God, their lives did not reflect the authentic attitude and actions of those who know and love God.

We're familiar with the phrase "Talk is cheap." We've been disappointed far too many times by parents who'd promise to play ball after work, but got busy; by guests who sent an RSVP, but never arrived; employees who slept in; spouses who vowed for better or for worse, but meant only *for better*; and pastors/priests who didn't practice what they publicly preached. The more often this happens, the more we are apt to respond in kind. We start to deceive ourselves into believing that words equal actions. As a result, we inevitably undermine trust in our relationships.

Jesus is asking us two things in today's coaching session. He's asking us to ponder why we say things to people that we do not really mean. He also encourages us to investigate whether our actions match what we say. His question, in effect, is, "Which son did the right thing, the one who said what the father wanted to hear or the son who did what his

Sometimes we say things to please people, to gain their acceptance, or to find temporary relief from their pressure. Beware of people who readily say yes. They are often available because they leave their previous commitments half done. Some who say no are those who finish what they begin and therefore do not take on tasks they cannot complete. People pleasers are willing to do whatever it takes to make others happy, compromising their character by saying things they don't mean. Jesus was telling us that what we say should coincide with what we do. Action is always a better indicator of character than talk. If you want to understand a person, don't interview him; just watch him in a variety of situations. We reveal ourselves most by our deeds.

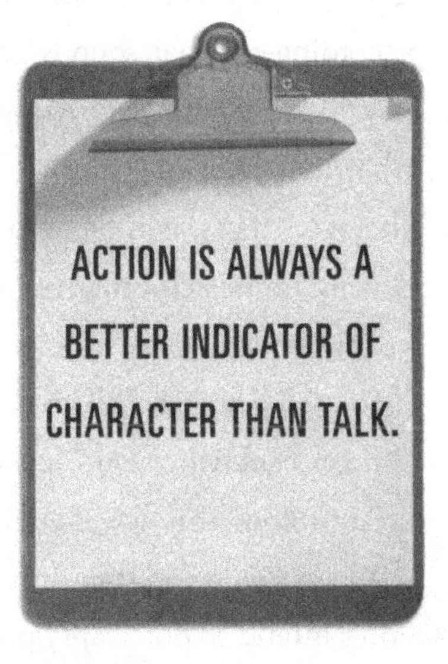
ACTION IS ALWAYS A
BETTER INDICATOR OF
CHARACTER THAN TALK.

"No" can be a painful answer with repercussions. By avoiding it we think we can escape its downside—but escape is temporary at best. Failing to follow through results in losing the respect of friends, coworkers, and supervisors. People begin to distrust you. While they rarely tell you this, they make a mental note and hedge their bets on you. Some will talk poorly about you, warning others to save disappointment by not counting on you. At work you can lose a promotion, raise, or other possible reward. You attract empty promises and lip service; people perceive that you don't value keeping your word, so you won't be bothered if they don't keep theirs. Some subtly punish you for letting them down.

The two best sources for monitoring your values are your calendar and your bank account. Where we spend our time and money are the strongest indicators of what motivates us. Questionnaires are unreliable. People tend to answer surveys according to what sounds good and what they believe they should say. We all want to appear good. But people tend to do what they honestly believe. The weak links in our chain, our character flaws, can be found where our speech and actions deviate from each other.

When you say yes, mean it. When you say no, mean that. If you tell a friend, "I'll give you a call," do it. When you say, "I'll get back with you," make sure you put it on your schedule to follow through. People count on you to do what you say. Don't fudge on the truth, tell white lies, or say things you don't intend to do. Empty promises come back to haunt you. After a while people won't trust you, and you'll wind up being lied to and deceived. You'll develop a jaded view of others, and you won't trust them, holding them at a distance and becoming friendless. If you don't do what you say, don't be disappointed when people drop the ball with you. You get what you give.

Every Sunday millions of people go to places of worship, recite verses, say prayers, and sing songs that would seem to profess an incredible faith in God. But what difference does faith make in their lives? It should transform the way they conduct business, do marriage, raise children, handle themselves in traffic, and invest time and money.

LET'S GET PERSONAL

It's obvious which son did the right thing. But sometimes when we're asked the obvious, we still hesitate to apply that trust to our own lives. Jesus's question today multiplies into three:

- Do you tend to tell people what they want to hear versus being honest with them?
- What areas of your life seem divided, where stated values do not reflect your lifestyle?
- Do your calendar and checkbook support what you profess about faith and values?

Today's coaching session encourages us to investigate our lives, looking for things we profess but don't live. Our faith is more an expression of what we do than what we say.

SESSION 13

LET'S GET GOING

1. How do you feel when people don't follow through with what they say? What can you learn from this?
2. Write down two or three specific actions you can take to align your speech with your action.
3. Name a current situation in which you've been doing more talking than acting. What is your action plan?

SESSION

14

ARE YOU A HERO?

Jesus said to them, "Why are you bothering this woman?"
—MATTHEW 26:10

Jesus's earthly work was winding down. His mind was probably preoccupied with a variety of matters regarding His pending crucifixion. While in the home of a friend, a woman quietly began anointing His feet with a very expensive perfume. The act was one of humility and gratitude. Obviously, Jesus had significantly impacted her life, and this was her way of saying thanks. Some of the "important" people in the room became nervous and uncomfortable with her expression of devotion and condemned her for spending money on a luxury item when the money could have been used to feed the poor.

While we may be shocked by the atrocities that take place

in war, psychological studies reveal how we are vulnerable to allowing evil to happen right under our own noses. When we sense we're in the minority, that we might be threatened by saying something, we don't want to buck the majority—then we turn dormant. Although we don't agree with the offense, we sit by idly—and so allow the birth of yet another victim.

The excuses of being too busy, of not wanting to stick your nose into other people's business, and of not risking involvement are just that: excuses. An excuse is a lie wrapped up in a reason. Jesus had earlier told His followers about the Good Samaritan, a story of only one passerby's stopping to intercede on behalf of a man who'd been mugged along the side of the road. In this situation Jesus was practicing what He preached: He was preventing a verbal mugging.

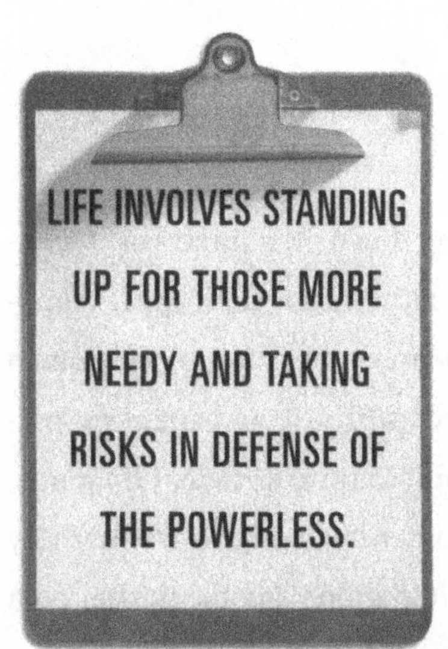
LIFE INVOLVES STANDING UP FOR THOSE MORE NEEDY AND TAKING RISKS IN DEFENSE OF THE POWERLESS.

Who do you stand up for in your work, at the grocery store, or at family events? Society is in need of heroes—and not the kind who ride in on white steeds necessarily, but the little ones in everyday life. Sticking up for a child, a single parent, the physically challenged, the mentally challenged, the poor and indigent, the elderly, or just the picked on—all are important causes. Don't let the ugly nature of others diminish your beauty. Stick up for the down-and-out and the easily intimidated. Life is not just about you. It involves standing up for those more needy and taking risks in defense of the powerless. Do right. Take time out of your busy schedule to be a hero to someone. Don't let the boldness or authority of others diminish your courage.

Bullies nearly always interrupt your schedule. They don't ask for permission to pick their prey. "What about the risk?" you might ask. Whistle-blowers are often fired these days. Good Samaritans still get sued. Sometimes the dog that you're defending bites you. Of course, defending someone may not require endangerment. Calling 911, sending an anonymous note to a supervisor, or moving behind the scenes to correct an injustice may be sufficient.

While the risk of sticking up for others is real, the potential rewards far outweigh the downside:

- You esteem the victim. Most victims are bullied frequently, not rarely. Your defense of them helps them to believe in their own value.

- You reduce the size of your bully. When people fail to stand up to those who take advantage of others, bullies begin to think they can get away with it. They do it more and more. By confronting the behavior, you interrupt the negative cycle.

- You feel good as a result. Although you may never receive a medal of valor, you feel the weight of one around your heart as you walk away. Doing right provides an internal reward.

- You please God. All through Scripture He is recognized as a defender of the powerless and victimized. That's part of His nature. When you exude the same quality, you demonstrate that you're "a chip off the old block." He'll smile on you.

- You provide a model. People are motivated by models. When one person stands up for the right thing, others are more apt to follow. Don't be the last one to join. Initiate the response. Most people need others to blaze the path. Be a leader.

- You get rewarded occasionally. That's not why you do it, but it's a nice by-product. Sometimes the reward is tangible; other times the reward comes later, in an indirect way.

LET'S GET PERSONAL

Jesus asks a question that is rhetorical. The answer was implied. He was saying, "Leave her alone. Get out of her face. Quit bugging her." The same question provides a powerful insight into our lives if we let it. Jesus is asking you three questions:

- When has someone rescued you?
- How do you stick up for people who are victimized, helpless, or bullied?
- Who in your life could use an advocate and defender right now?

In today's coaching session Jesus is asking you to ponder the importance of caring for the powerless. Whether it's defending people who're being talked about in their absence or saying something to an adult who cuts in front of a child in the grocery line, look out for others. The needy person probably won't ask for your help. Many of them are used to being picked on. They're accustomed to people's passing them by as if they don't matter. But they do matter. Make a difference in the life of a person who's apt to be impacted by your effort.

LET'S GET GOING

1. When have you come to someone's rescue?
2. What is a small, everyday example of how you might champion someone who is being harassed, ridiculed, or intimidated? Write a specific to-do goal.
3. Why do you think so few people take the risk to stand up to those who would pick on others? Read aloud, "I vow to champion the weak and defenseless."

SESSION

15

WHY ARE YOU AFRAID?

> *He replied, "You of little faith, why are you so afraid?" Then he got up and rebuked the winds and the waves, and it was completely calm.*
>
> —MATTHEW 8:26

We're more apt to learn in certain situations than others. These are called teachable moments. In between these fertile times life learning is less productive. Jesus coached His small cadre of followers 24/7, allowing Him to seize teachable moments as they occurred. One of those moments came in the middle of a large lake, during a violent storm. In spite of the recent miracles they'd seen Jesus perform, present conditions intimidated them. Jesus was asleep in the boat, seemingly oblivious to their plight. Because they could not control their circumstances, they feared. Who could blame them? They might drown!

Psychologists tell us that most people are primarily externally oriented. If you were to eavesdrop on office dialogue or coffee shop conversations, you'd likely hear something like this:

"How are you doing?"

"Oh, just great . . . The weather's so nice . . . I got a raise . . . My child brought home a good report card . . . We're going on vacation next week . . . I lost two pounds . . ."

But when circumstances are less than optimum, we can find ample reasons to be down. "How are you doing?"

"Oh, I've been better . . . It's so rainy today . . . The stock market's down . . . Traffic is a bear . . . Can you believe her attitude . . . He makes me so mad . . ."

Fear is what we feel when we sense we're not in control. It is nearly always in terms of degrees.

FEAR CONTINUUM

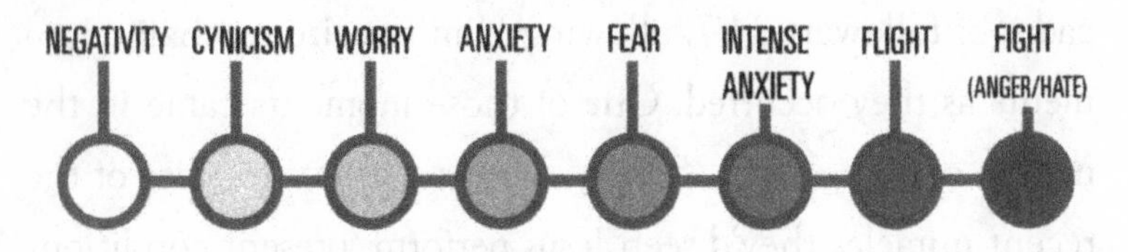

On the fear continuum low-grade fear is expressed as negativity. As a general rule negative people are more fearful than merely pessimistic people. They disguise their fear in cynicism, finding it socially acceptable that way. Next come worry and anxiety. Worry usually reflects a specific fear; anxiety a more overarching one. Next in intensity is what we commonly denote as fear and intense anxiety, moving toward the flight or fight response. Concentrated fear is often disguised as anger and hatred. Therefore, the opposite of love is not so much hatred as it is fear. "Perfect love drives out fear" (1 John 4:18).

Is your daily life fear based or faith based? Because of our five senses, we're tempted to rely predominately on external conditions for feedback, reacting to what we perceive. An internal response mechanism is faith, which does not deny circumstances but transcends them. Faith looks at things, not as they are, but as they may become, positively. Fear is actually faith in the negative, anticipating an adverse outcome. Faith has the ability to create what it focuses on, fear-oriented people actually attract what they fear. Consider faith a magnet, whether positive or negative. When faith is placed in God who is sovereign, then no set of circumstances is invincible. We're never totally powerless with faith; we have the ability to remain at peace, in spite of the situation.

We often choose fear without realizing it. We justify it logically. "Look at the waves; hear the wind moan; feel the boat rock. We're doomed." Our expressions reveal our orientation. One way to detect fear is to monitor your speech.

Listen to what you say. Fear-laced statements include: "I'm afraid . . ." "What if we don't make it?" "I can always go back." "If it doesn't work out . . ." "I'm worried that . . ." "We can't . . ." Faith is also reflected in speech. Faith expressions include: "I can . . ." "God can help us." "I think we could . . ." "Yes, let's . . ." "It's going to be all right." "God's in charge." "If it's His will . . ."

Faith circuit breakers can make it difficult for us to hang on to faith. These include past conditioning, such as pain, failure, the negative influence of others, and fear modeling. Instead of succumbing to fear at increasingly high voltage, we're apt to give up on faith at low voltage. Of course, we don't consider it meaningless. We easily justify our abandonment of faith. "Just look for yourself at the waves around me and the wind blowing in my face. It's a storm, and I'm out in a boat in the middle of the lake." Sometimes we even find comfort in these negative consolations. We consider them a license to complain and quit. But Jesus encourages us to stop excusing our fear response and to choose faith.

LET'S GET PERSONAL

The men are terrified of a mighty storm in which they believe they will die. I get that! But Jesus uses this as a teaching moment and asks a tough question. He asks you three questions in today's coaching session:

- What situations do you tend to face with fear?

- What are the pros and cons of basing your responses on external circumstances?

- What is likely to occur, and how can you handle the outcomes with faith?

There is a negative correlation between fear and faith. While some people seem more predisposed to fear and others to exude faith, the latter is the means to the optimum life. Some of us must work harder at it than others, but faith is right for everyone. Imagine faith and fear as opposite ends of a tug of war. You must decide which end of the rope you're going to be on so that you can pull in that direction. Your response will alter your feelings and can change the outcome. Speak faith. Act out of hope. Face life from an inner, spiritual perspective instead of an external, physical orientation.

LET'S GET GOING

1. How are your feelings of anger and fear associated with each other?

2. What words do you use to communicate your faith or fear?

3. List four things you can do to focus more on faith today.

SESSION

16

WHO IS YOUR ROLE MODEL?

He also told them this parable: "Can a blind man lead a blind man? Will they not both fall into a pit? A student is not above his teacher, but everyone who is fully trained will be like his teacher."

—LUKE 6:39–40

The great poet John Donne has told us that no man is an island. We're all influenced by those who have marked our lives, positively and negatively, while we were children, adolescents, young adults, and adults. Our lives are a compilation of those who've impressed us with their actions, teachings, values, and lifestyles. A small handful of individuals rise to the top in terms of influencing how we live. To assume that we're "our own person" is both naive and egotistical. No one escapes the impressions of significant others in their past and present.

Determining who it is that speaks into your life is an important matter. Think twice before enlisting a marriage counselor who is divorced or never married. Beware of an out-of-shape fitness trainer. Avoid a cardiologist who smokes. Question a future mate who does not share your core values. Ask your business consultant if he's been in a situation like yours. Ponder how the values of the people giving you advice emulate the kind of life that you want to eventually possess. The blind spots in others lead us down paths that are apt to be rocky and dangerous. The man who cares little about the morals of the leader whom he follows is foolish. The woman taking advice from a friend who does not walk her talk is destined for problems. Expertise in one area does not necessarily overflow into other areas.

Who are you following? Consider the books you are reading. Do a little investigation into the authors' backgrounds. Think about the person who recommended each book. Take inventory of the qualities of those who speak into your life and with whom you interact on a regular basis. Do not be so foolish as to say your concrete is hardened, your die is cast, you're immune to the influences of others. You're not. While you can't avoid "blind men" in your life altogether, you need to assess their weaknesses. Try to be aware of the blindness of those whom you read, listen to, and hang around. None of us is void of blind spots. Lack of recognition of the shortcomings of those who influence you will make you vulnerable.

As we get old enough not to need an actual model, we should think more in terms of path than pedestrian. Our goal is not to emulate others as much as it is to follow their path and learn from them. Note how they are similar and dissimilar to you. Consider what it is about them that puts a good light on the path you're taking. Think about what might be detrimental if you are to do as they do or believe as they believe.

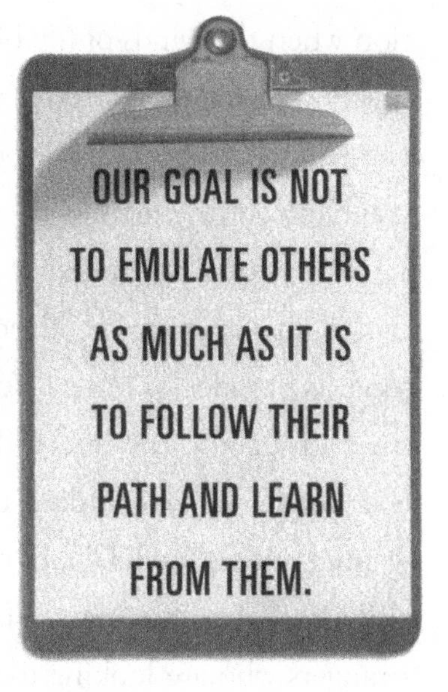
OUR GOAL IS NOT
TO EMULATE OTHERS
AS MUCH AS IT IS
TO FOLLOW THEIR
PATH AND LEARN
FROM THEM.

Scripture instructs us not to be "unequally yoked" with a person whose core values are different from ours. While this is a peer relationship versus mentorship, the bigger issue here is about partnering. The yoke metaphor is that of two animals placed in a wooden harness, pulling a plow or heavy weight. If you put unequal animals together, such as a donkey and an ox, or a sheep and a mule, or a horse and a camel, you'll have problems. The significant difference in terms of orientation will make the plowing difficult.

Whether it's business, marriage, friendship, or partnering in any significant endeavor, make sure you're on the same frequency in terms of values. Investigate a person's concept of God, morality, and lifestyle. Don't take these for granted. These core matters set a person's sail, establishing the direction when the winds of life blow. Yoke up with someone who shares your values, or better yet, someone whom you respect and admire. Good or bad, you become like those with whom you hang out the most.

If it is true that none of us is an island, this also means that right or wrong, good or bad, intentionally or not, you serve as a model for others. Your life leads others further down the path or into the ditch. "But I never bargained for that," you admit. "I never asked to be someone's guide. I never wanted to be a model." Ah, but you are. You have neighbors, children, work associates, family members, and complete strangers who are looking to you for cues as to how you deal with problems, difficult people, and decision making. They watch and learn. Some of them will quote you, follow your example, and set their course based on your model. You need not be the president of a large corporation, a minister, or public-school teacher. You cannot *not* influence. The questions are then, "Where do you lead people? What do they learn from you? How do you steer them forward, sideways, or backward with your life?"

LET'S GET PERSONAL

Jesus was again asking His students a rhetorical question. He answered it Himself since it deserved more than a mere yes or no. But His question serves as a premise for our coaching session today.

- Who do you look toward as a model, mentor, or teacher; is that person reliable?
- Do you share core values with those to whom you're considering forming a partnership or close tie?
- Who are you influencing, and what kind of model are you providing?

In today's coaching session, Jesus is raising the matter of influence. You are never too old to have a model and never to young to serve as one. Consider who it is you look up to and who looks up to you. You are being watched, with or without your blessing. Someone is being influenced by your vision and by your blindness. Think about what you need to do to improve the quality of the people who speak into your life, and what you should do to become a better guide for others.

SESSION 16

LET'S GET GOING

1. Name a person whom you are following or who is influencing you. What are the strengths and weaknesses of this person?

2. How do your values overlap or contradict your significant other? Your business partner? Your boss?

3. For whom are you a model, mentor, or teacher? List two or three things you can do to improve the quality of your influence.

SESSION

HOW DO YOU GET PEOPLE TO LOVE YOU MORE?

"Two men owed money to a certain moneylender. One owed him five hundred denarii, and the other fifty. Neither of them had the money to pay him back, so he canceled the debts of both. Now which of them will love him more?"

—LUKE 7:41–42

Today's coaching session has to do with gratitude and motivation. Jesus used this story to explain why a woman with a bad reputation was washing His feet at a social function. She'd experienced forgiveness for a very carnal lifestyle and thus felt far more appreciation than others in the room. She was motivated to honor Jesus and thank Him. Jesus touches on the secret of gratitude and human motivation in this brief lesson. People feel appreciation toward those who are gracious to them. Charisma is not just a personality wiring. It's also a skill that can be cultivated so that others are drawn to us.

The first lesson has to do with the intensity of our gratitude in life. The world is full of ungrateful people who are smug in self-righteousness. Their lack of humility is based on the presumption that they have little moral debt. In other words, they feel that life owes them more than they owe life.

Ingratitude can be masked by superficial manners. We may say please and thank you without truly being appreciative. An attitude of gratitude transcends mere etiquette. A person who is authentically and consistently gracious is self-aware. He has met his failures face-on and embraced them. Those who deny or avoid their imperfections are prone to exude a haughty disposition. "I don't need grace. I'm good enough on my own."

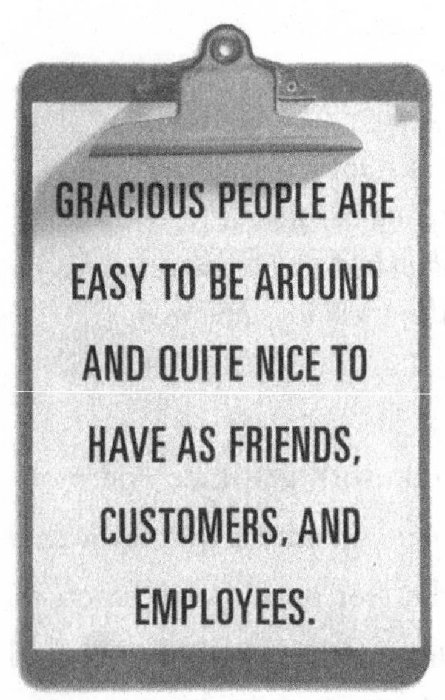
GRACIOUS PEOPLE ARE EASY TO BE AROUND AND QUITE NICE TO HAVE AS FRIENDS, CUSTOMERS, AND EMPLOYEES.

An underdeveloped sense of appreciation underlies numerous attitude offspring, such as criticism, anger, bitterness, revenge, and pride. "I'm entitled. I deserve some attention. How dare you treat me this way? Do you know who I am? What's your problem? Why can't you perform better?"

Gracious people understand where they've come from and accept their imperfections. They know they've benefited from countless acts of charity in spite of their actions. They know that without the forgiveness of God and others, they would be in eternal bondage of emotional debts they could never repay.

While living in the past is not healthy, periodically opening our flaw file has a way of keeping us humble. (Looking at our own flaw file also prevents others from feeling the need to do so.) Count the times you've received grace. How quickly we forget. Mature people are able to weave humility out of their faults, turning rags into riches. Let past failures motivate you to respond to life with grace and appreciation. Never assume you're entitled.

Having filed for spiritual bankruptcy, gracious people are pliable, gentle, and kind. They smile sooner and longer than the unrepentant. They dole out grace to others faster and in greater proportions than the rest. They're low maintenance. They are easy to be around and quite nice to have as friends, customers, and employees. People are fond of them.

Jesus asks you to consider the gifts of grace you've unwrapped, many unknowingly. God has granted you scores of second chances. Think of all the situations where you've performed poorly, created messes, and failed. Use these memories not to feel bad or to grovel in self-deprecation, but to ignite a spirit of humility and grateful praise.

The act of forgiveness serves as a powerful motivator.

People who've experienced acceptance and second chances from you are far more apt to feel indebted to you. They are drawn to you. They want to be with people who see beyond their failures and continue to believe in them. Although exceptions to the rule exist, count on finding gracious people at the end of your expressions of forgiveness. We have little tolerance for those who treat us poorly. A lack of forgiveness demotivates. People spurn those who judge them.

The world is full of people who never offer second chances. They are unforgiving, demanding, and difficult to please. The person who does extend grace stands out in a crowd and doesn't respond to hurts and failures like everyone else. Chances are your fans include those who've received your love, acceptance, and forgiveness. These mark a gracious person's life.

LET'S GET PERSONAL

Jesus is not trying to train His followers to love only those who have something to give. He is simply teaching a principle based on human temperament. Jesus asks us to consider three questions through today's session:

- How can you develop a more gracious attitude by remembering the times you've taxed the patience and grace of others?

- To whom do you need to extend a second chance without using it as a tool for manipulation?

- What can you do to turn others' failures into positive energy of appreciation for you?

To become known as a grace giver is a worthwhile endeavor that yields many benefits to you and the recipients of your goodness. Grace receiving and giving impact your effectiveness with others.

LET'S GET GOING

1. Name a time you messed up or failed significantly.
2. Who forgave you or gave you a second chance?
3. Who in your life can use forgiveness, and how can you communicate this?

SESSION

WHO NEEDS YOU?

As Jesus was on his way, the crowds almost crushed him. And a woman was there who had been subject to bleeding for twelve years, but no one could heal her. She came up behind him and touched the edge of his cloak, and immediately her bleeding stopped.

"Who touched me?" Jesus asked.

—Luke 8:42–45

People, people everywhere. A majority of our lives is spent with others in elevators, restaurants, malls, offices, churches, parks, and on freeways. Most of us are consistently being bombarded with voice mails, pages, e-mails, letters, text messages, meetings, and phone calls. Today's coaching session has to do with being attentive to unique opportunities that are often neglected.

Jesus was a popular personality in the short years that He

taught, healed, and interacted with people. On various occasions He had to escape pressing crowds in order to be alone. He was constantly hounded by those who wanted to meet and be touched by Him. On one occasion He was pushing through a crowd, when a woman squeezed through arms and legs in order to touch the hem of His robe. Suddenly Jesus stopped and asked, "Who touched Me?"

The normal path of our daily lives may include countless interactions with business associates, clients, family members, strangers, and friends. The intellectual response is: "Everyone's trying to get a piece of me." The more intuitive response causes us to look at people differently, "Someone I'll meet today needs my touch. They are seeking more than a professional response." On occasion people cross our paths who need our special attention. Be aware. Notice. Listen to your heart. Respond to your intuitions. By listening to your heart, you can discern those whom God has sent.

This quest may be too mystical for some. Intellectual types may feel defensive about the concept that we ought to utilize our sixth sense. As an important person of His day, Jesus might have understandably not possessed this sensitivity, but He did. He was good with people because He noticed what others did not.

First of all, be cognizant of the inconspicuous touches. Notice the janitor down the hall taking out the trash or cleaning one of the public rest rooms. Thank him. Tell him you appreciate his work. When you go through a secretary to talk to a manager, compliment the way she answers the phone or wish her a good day. When you go out to eat, look the hostess in the eyes and extend a grateful smile. Notice the "small people" in your life who often go unnoticed either because you don't interact with them physically or because you're preoccupied with another agenda. Run to the garbage collector and hand him an appreciation note with a Starbucks card enclosed. Put a "we love our mail deliverer" letter in the mailbox. See the behind-the-scene people. Look for those who go unnoticed by the masses, lost in the crowds.

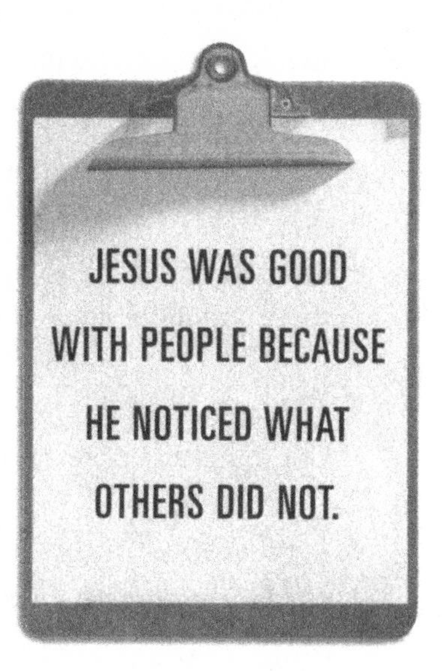
JESUS WAS GOOD
WITH PEOPLE BECAUSE
HE NOTICED WHAT
OTHERS DID NOT.

By looking for these quiet touches, you learn humility. Life does not revolve around you. Numerous people provide you with the food you buy, the clothes you wear, the roads you drive, and any number of things you experience every day. By seeing the complex web of people working together, you discover a new appreciation for all you have.

Next, believe that God has certain people He wants to touch through you, people He'll bring into your life on a daily basis. While these folks may not schedule appointments, anticipate at least one or two a day so that your radar will be operating for you to notice them. It may be an employee who hints at a difficult family situation. It may be one of your children who needs a private date with you. It could be a neighbor, when you "happen" to meet at the mailbox. Don't go overboard, approaching everyone as if they're God's project for you. But realize that a few of them will need a special touch.

That touch might result in any number of things. Perhaps someone needs a listening ear, a task to be performed, money, a recommendation, or a helping hand. Listen to your inner voice. Take the risk to stop and ask the question, "Who touched me?" As you take the time to do this, you'll discover three things:

- Your intuition will get better. You'll be able to discern those unique voices from the swirling crowds'.
- You'll be fulfilled. To meet a human need and be used by God is a very rewarding adventure.
- You'll inevitably reap what you sow. When you have needs, the law of sowing and reaping will bring good things to you.

LET'S GET PERSONAL

The feedback Jesus got from His disciples was more intellectual than intuitive. "What do you mean who touched You? We're walking down these narrow village streets; everyone is pushing against You; and You ask the question, 'Who touched

Me?'" But Jesus knew what we often overlook: that all touches are not the same. The question He asked was originally to those around Him, but right now it's to you.

His question can be expanded into three main points.

- Who do you need to stop and recognize in your busy schedule?
- Who are the stealth people in your life who may be easy to ignore?
- How can you be more sensitive to the divine appointments God has prepared for you?

Today's coaching session calls you to look for those who touch your life in unique ways. Your ability to sense these opportunities and respond appropriately will add a wonderful new dimension to your life.

LET'S GET GOING

1. List three or four people in your spheres of influence who touch your life on a regular basis but usually go unnoticed.
2. List one response you can make this next week to each of those you listed above.
3. What may be blocking your intuitive skills for sensing these special individuals?

Me?" But Jesus knew what we often overlook: that all [illegible] are not the same. The question He asked was origi[illegible] [illegible] expand [illegible]

The question can be expanded into [illegible]

* Who [illegible] need [illegible] schedule?

* Who [illegible] in your life who [illegible] [illegible]?

* [illegible] the [illegible] ments [illegible] the world?

[illegible] [illegible] those who [illegible] [illegible]

LET'S GET GOING

[illegible] three or four people [illegible] [illegible] [illegible] regularly [illegible] [illegible]

[illegible] this next week to reach [illegible]

[illegible] these [illegible]

SESSION

19

WHAT DO YOU KNOW?

On one occasion an expert in the law stood up to test Jesus. "Teacher," he asked, "what must I do to inherit eternal life?"

"What is written in the Law?" he replied. "How do you read it?"

He answered: "'Love the Lord your God with all your heart and with all your soul and with all your strength and with all your mind'; and, 'Love your neighbor as yourself.'"

—LUKE 10:25–27

One definition of sin in the Bible is knowing the good we should do but doing nothing about it (see James 4:17). Sometimes having another person hold us accountable to act upon what we already know raises our confidence level. We often know what we need to do, but we don't act on it. Jesus was acting as an outside consultant, saying, "Come on, don't pretend you don't know the answer. You know what you need to do. Face it. Be honest with yourself." There are five categories regarding knowledge and self-awareness:

1. You know and know you know (confidence).
2. You know and do not know that you know (lack of confidence and self-awareness).
3. You don't know and know you don't know (acknowledged ignorance).
4. You don't know and don't know that you don't know (blind spot).
5. You think you know, but don't know (foolishness/unreliable confidence).

The scholar apparently needed someone to help him tap into what he already knew. None of us can be all we need to be by ourselves. Consider finding a coach. Tap a friend who can hold you accountable. Ask a mentor to help you be responsible for what you already know. Don't be ashamed to seek the assistance of someone else. Jesus never shamed the scholar for posing the question. Sometimes hearing what we already know raises our confidence level. At other times we benefit most by having someone who can help us avoid playing games.

The scholar asked Jesus a question. Jesus turned it around and said in essence, "You're a smart guy. You tell me." Sometimes we try to rescue people instead of helping them confront what they already know. Giving them an answer can be easier than helping them articulate the answer for themselves. The latter response results in far greater ownership, which in turn raises the likelihood of action. Skirting responsibility is a favorite pastime of many people. We'd rather shop for exercise clothes than work out. We'd prefer to read about personal finances than establish a budget. We'd just as soon criticize a political decision than go serve a meal to the homeless. We'd rather debate the existence of God than worship Him. Merely reading the instructions won't assemble the apparatus.

Mark Twain said, "It's not what I don't understand in the Bible that bothers me. It's what I do." Be careful not to confuse knowledge with action. Awareness is different than behavior. We can use others to hold us accountable for what we already know. Jesus did this for the scholar in a nonthreatening way, even though we can imagine how disconcerting it may have been for the scholar to answer his own question. He couldn't hide behind his lack of confidence or feigned ignorance anymore. Did he feel embarrassed that he already knew the answer to the question he'd asked? The bigger mystery is, now that he knew, would he act on his knowledge?

LET'S GET PERSONAL

What was already in the man's head had not made it to his heart, the symbolic seat of will and action. The man knew the answer, but apparently was not living it. Jesus's coaching session is a great way for us to confront similar inconsistencies in ourselves.

- Do you have convictions that you can't seem to live out?
- Who is holding you responsible for living up to your potential?
- Are you helping anyone connect mental knowledge with practical application?

In today's coaching session Jesus is asking you to act on what you already know. What inconsistencies are keeping you from reaching your potential? It's not always what we don't know that keeps us back; it could be failing to act on what we already know. Truth not acted upon is wasted.

LET'S GET GOING

1. If you were consulting with someone in your situation, what would you tell him or her?
2. Who is holding you responsible for applying what you know?
3. Who are you helping to be responsible for doing what they know?

SESSION

20

HOW MUCH DOES IT COST?

"Suppose one of you wants to build a tower. Will he not first sit down and estimate the cost to see if he has enough money to complete it? For if he lays the foundation and is not able to finish it, everyone who sees it will ridicule him, saying, 'This fellow began to build and was not able to finish.'

"Or suppose a king is about to go to war against another king. Will he not first sit down and consider whether he is able with ten thousand men to oppose the one coming against him with twenty thousand? If he is not able, he will send a delegation while the other is still a long way off and will ask for terms of peace. In the same way, any of you who does not give up everything he has cannot be my disciple."

—LUKE 14:28–33

Everyone is wired differently; we make decisions in various ways. Some of us are spur-of-the-moment, shoot-from-the-hip folks who spontaneously make commitments without thinking through the details. The cry of this person is "No fear!" These people often do amazing things because they loathe the status quo. However, they may also have the tendency to give up when things are no longer fun or intriguing.

On the other end of the decision-making spectrum is the cautious crew. "We won't launch into a new venture until we have assessed every risk, pondered the payoffs, and considered the unknowns. We pursue only opportunities that seem to be slam dunks." These people have things under control. However, they try to be masters of their universes, which is really impossible.

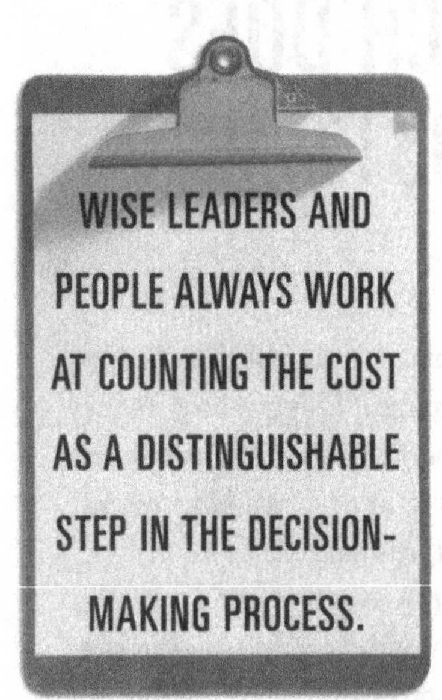
WISE LEADERS AND PEOPLE ALWAYS WORK AT COUNTING THE COST AS A DISTINGUISHABLE STEP IN THE DECISION-MAKING PROCESS.

Today's coaching session deals with the process by which you personally go about assessing the pros and cons before you make a commitment. When you think about it, your current place in life is primarily a result of the decisions you've made in the past. Improve your decision-making skills and you improve your life. Fail to excel in this area and you run the risk of wasting your life. Jesus used two examples in His teaching in Luke 14. He talked about a person constructing a tower who investigates the design, cost of materials and labor, soil types, and any number of other related details. This person doesn't want to get started only to have to quit, losing all that he's put into it—not to mention his credibility.

The other example Jesus gave is of a king who is about to go to war with a neighboring army. He'd better not let his pride get in front of the process, or he's apt to lose both his military as well as his throne. A prudent king tries to estimate whether or not he can win so that he'll have time to negotiate a peace treaty. Wise leaders and people always work at counting the cost as a distinguishable step in the decision-making process.

Obviously, all decisions are not created equal. Some have more devastating effects if we take them lightly, and others are far less important. You probably don't need to count the cost in terms of the color of shirt you wear or what gas station you choose to fill your tank. People tend to make mistakes, however, when they underestimate important decisions. By taking a moment to assess how a letter you are writing may seem, or how a confrontational e-mail you're sending might be taken, or what the ramifications of a long-term lease will do to your cash flow, you can save yourself significant headaches. "A stitch in time saves nine" refers to taking time to sew well so that you don't have to waste more time later fixing a problem.

When we fail to weigh the gravity of a decision, we often waste precious resources. First, establish the challenges you're facing today. Next, consider which of them should require extra thought and effort so that you don't underestimate them. Think about which ones will shrink if postponed and which will grow.

Once you've determined the medium and more crucial decisions, you need to weigh the costs—in terms of talent, time, money, and material. Every decision carries an emotional price tag. Inventory your resources. Factor in the worst-case scenario if you do not make the commitment. Include what you might lose in reputation, money, time, and emotions.

Hindsight is more accurate than foresight, but there are ways of increasing your foresight. Four of these ways include:

Your Experience: Past lessons give you a perspective on estimating the upside and downside of this challenge. Don't force yourself to relearn life lessons.

Others' Experience: Seek input from someone who's been down this road. Consultants and mentors are invaluable when it comes to providing key experiences that will help you make informed decisions.

Peer Ideas: Two heads are better than one; three or four are best. Find a small group that can hear your ideas and then give you alternatives and fresh perspectives.

Reflective Intuition: Most decisions we need to make have a gestation period that allows you to ponder costs, relax, and then come to a conclusion. Let your heart do some of the work, not just your head. The "gut" can be a good barometer, as our digestive system is connected with our conscious and subconscious emotional states.

LET'S GET PERSONAL

Jesus often told stories. And He often taught the moral of the story by asking a question. He does the same with today's question. Three questions spring from the one:

- How do you go about weighing the importance of a decision?
- How do you assess the costs and payoffs before making a commitment?
- What might you be overlooking in your estimate and why?

Today Jesus is teaching you to make decisions wisely, so that you can follow through on your commitments. The goal of thorough investigation is not to deter you from making a decision but to help you be successful in it.

LET'S GET GOING

1. What are two small, two medium, and two large decisions you're facing?
2. What will the medium and large issues cost you in terms of time, resources, emotions, and effort?
3. What are the potential downsides if you don't take these seriously or if you underestimate the costs?

SESSION

WHAT'S IN YOUR EPITAPH?

And he told them this parable: "The ground of a certain rich man produced a good crop. He thought to himself, 'What shall I do? I have no place to store my crops.'

"Then he said, 'This is what I'll do. I will tear down my barns and build bigger ones, and there I will store all my grain and my goods. And I'll say to myself, "You have plenty of good things laid up for many years. Take life easy; eat, drink and be merry."'

"But God said to him, 'You fool! This very night your life will be demanded from you. Then who will get what you have prepared for yourself?'"

—LUKE 12:16–20

The best way to live in the present is to have a proper perspective on the future. When you fail to develop a belief for the beyond, you'll tend to wander through the here and now. An airplane without a destination is apt to roam around the skies like a butterfly on a breezy day. In today's coaching session Jesus calls on you to consider the provocative topic of . . . your death. Ironically, gazing at the end improves your vision of the immediate. You can't take anything with you, but everyone leaves a legacy. What kind of legacy are you leaving? Imagine eavesdropping on your memorial service. The mourners' discussions will reflect the true impact you made during your brief trek on this terrestrial ball. Visualize things about yourself that people will and will not miss six months after you're dead. Think about who'll visit your grave on significant days.

CONSIDER THE ENDURING
VALUE OF THINGS
YOU'RE LEAVING BEHIND.

Consider the enduring value of things you'll leave behind. They tend to be the items least mentioned in wills, things such as elevated self-esteems of those who interacted with you, fond memories of those you've served, protégés you've mentored, motivated teammates, and a handful of close friends. Think about the qualities of family members you'll leave behind. Consider how your kids, spouse, and siblings will remember you.

Throughout history people have taken the conventional approach to success: money, power, fame, and pleasure. Your values and priorities reflect what is most meaningful to you. Note that Jesus does not malign the reality of having things as much as He condemns man's attitude toward them: "Fool!" Money, power, notoriety, popularity, and abilities are tools, not goals; they are means, not ends. When you treat them as final objectives, you'll wind up broke, no matter the appraised value of your estate.

When a person buys into the external realm for life achievement, a natural by-product is the quantity road: more, bigger, faster, nicer. It's the bigger-barn syndrome. While some suggest that their goal is quality more than quantity, what they usually mean is more niceness, more taste, more speed, more beauty. The insatiable appetite for more pushes budgets beyond their boundaries and employees to the precipice of burnout, not to mention the need for extensive maintenance. We fool ourselves into believing that the goal is to eventually rest and enjoy it, but this rarely happens. The treadmill is difficult to dismount.

Most people procrastinate planning for their exit. Nearly everyone with perceived good health anticipates years more of living. Psychologists say that it is very difficult for us to contemplate our deaths. Because the perceived supply of time is great, we do not value it as we might otherwise. "I'll plan for the end later. I've got plenty of time. I don't need to worry about death. Eternity seems like an eternity away." Psychologists have a word for this way of thinking—denial.

LET'S GET PERSONAL

This lesson was originally the result of Jesus's being asked to resolve an inheritance dispute between two brothers. Realizing the man was asking the wrong question, Jesus gave him something far more valuable: an insight on living. He asks of the man, and of us:

- What are you leaving behind?
- What are you trying to build with your life?
- What are you doing today with eternity in mind?

A healthy anticipation of one's death is not a morbid, fear-inducing attitude that pollutes our daily lives. Quite the opposite is true. People who regularly ponder the brevity of their years cultivate the unique ability to focus on what matters most. Life is either the main event or a rehearsal for the main event. Your decision will determine what you value and how you live. If we prepare for eternity and none exists, we risk little. If, on the other hand, we live only for today, when in fact we're on the front porch of eternity, we may miss it all.

Jesus leaves us with an internal bombshell, set to go off by a crisis. It may be a car accident, a bad health diagnosis, divorce, bankruptcy, firing, or midlife confusion. Unfortunately for the man in Jesus's story, his priority-startling event was death. By then it's too late to change values. Today is your opportunity to take the road less traveled; rearrange appropriately. Invest in what won't blow away with the wind of culture and time. Pursue what is apt to endure the longest. Eternity is not a matter of classroom philosophizing, but a motivator for how we spend our money, what we do with our time, and the sort of relationships we foster.

LET'S GET GOING

1. What are you investing in with your life?
2. How might your epitaph read if you died today? How would you like it to read?
3. Based on these thoughts, what do you want to do more? Less?

SESSION

22

IS PEACE ALWAYS THE GOAL?

I have come to bring fire on the earth, and how I wish it were already kindled! But I have a baptism to undergo, and how distressed I am until it is completed! Do you think I came to bring peace on earth? No, I tell you, but division.
—LUKE 12:49–51

Every individual will at times be called to do things that are apt to create a stir. We will have to take risks for a greater cause. Sometimes, standing for what is right will make things worse: Differences of opinions can create uncomfortable stress in families and organizations. Confronting wayward friends steals countless hours of sleep. Taking a stand that is unpopular makes us feel stupid. But if we shrink from these situations in order to prolong peace, we'll end up hurting ourselves and others by our lack of courage. Consider the firefighter who sometimes starts fires in order to reduce the risk of a larger, uncontrollable burn; likewise, every one of us must at times create some heat when responsibility falls on us to catalyze change. Those of us unwilling to buck the tide, to stand up for a right, though unpopular, belief, or to confront an erring leader or team member do little to benefit society.

When you become aware of an issue that needs to be confronted and you see that no one else is responding, the job may fall on you. When others do not see an important problem, the situation might call for a prophet. The proverb of the little boy who told the emperor that he was naked illustrates the need for truth tellers. You can't assume that because others are silent, they are enlightened, honest . . . or loyal.

The athlete gets irritated by the coach who reminds him he must awaken early to run in the cold, dark hours. The drunk screams at the family members who say no to more money for booze. The rebellious teen gets angry with the parent for establishing a curfew. The cantankerous two-year-old throws a fit because her mother forces her to sit in the high chair. The seasoned politician raises the ire of voters for turning down a bill, that he believes will harm constituents. The employee is "let go" for holding a superior accountable for cheating on an expense reimbursement. These are a few examples of everyday situations where sparks were created by doing the right thing. Shaking up the status quo can get you fired, threatened, or even nailed to a cross. We have to know what lines to draw and when to draw them, otherwise we're little more than troublemakers. The person who can't get along with others or perpetually picks fights doesn't understand what Jesus is talking about here. The wisdom is in knowing what to be willing to fight about.

LET'S GET PERSONAL

Is this the same person who preached, "Blessed are the peacemakers"? How did Jesus justify this radical agenda amidst His other teachings on love, compassion, and tending to the needs of others? Despite the stereotypes people have of Jesus, He never advocated passivity. Jesus was an agent of change. Today's coaching session is about understanding the need to create tension at strategic times.

- Are you aware of a situation that needs to be confronted?
- Is any of your desire to keep the peace unhealthy?
- Are you willing to take a stand for what's right if it means risking being let go, losing a friendship, or giving up your security?

We can't always predict the outcomes. Change has no guarantees. Leaving the security of the present does not mean you'll land safely on the banks of tomorrow. Don't confuse a secure feeling with doing what is right.

If after considering these questions you find yourself unwilling to take a stand that is needed, another set of questions is appropriate. Why are you unwilling to confront a problem? What is holding you back? Do you have your interests in mind, or are you thinking about the welfare of others? Do you value your security more than you do the positive outcomes of confronting an evil? Why do you fear? What bad experience in your past has made you resistant to taking a stand?

Jesus teaches us that at times peacekeeping is evil. In the proper situations your right actions will spawn tension and division. Don't let that keep you from doing what is right. While this is not a license to be insensitive, disloyal, or overly confrontational, wisdom is in knowing when to pick a fight and when to pursue peace.

LET'S GET GOING

1. List several matters that deserve confrontation in your life.

2. What is keeping you from taking an appropriate stand?

3. What are the downsides of risking division? What are the potential benefits?

SESSION

ARE YOU NEIGHBORLY?

On one occasion an expert in the law stood up to test Jesus. . . . "And who is my neighbor?"

In reply Jesus said: "A man was going down from Jerusalem to Jericho, when he fell into the hands of robbers. They stripped him of his clothes, beat him and went away, leaving him half dead. A priest happened to be going down the same road, and when he saw the man, he passed by on the other side. So too, a Levite, when he came to the place and saw him, passed by on the other side. But a Samaritan, as he traveled, came where the man was; and when he saw him, he took pity on him. He went to him and bandaged his wounds, pouring on oil and wine. Then he put the man on his own donkey, took him to an inn and took care of him. The next day he took out two silver coins and gave them to the innkeeper. 'Look after him,' he said, 'and when I return, I will reimburse you for any extra expense you may have.'

"Which of these three do you think was a neighbor to the man who fell into the hands of robbers?"

The expert in the law replied, "The one who had mercy on him."

Jesus told him, "Go and do likewise."

—LUKE 10:25, 29–37

Have you ever heard a master politician being interviewed by the media? The good ones are incredibly adept at avoiding the difficult questions by responding with generalities and taking the opportunity to spin the conversation to their advantage. The ability to take a heated question and deactivate its lethal potential is a powerful ability. But in today's coaching session, we see Jesus doing the opposite. Unlike a good politician, He takes a passive question of a bystander and puts a rather provocative twist to it, making it more powerful and poignant than the original.

An astute, religious man came to Jesus and asked Him a popular, philosophical question of his day, "Who is my neighbor?" Jesus responds with a story that may have been a revision of the day's news, regarding a man who was mugged along a stretch of desert known as the Red Way. It was named that for the amount of blood that was spilled there by thugs and thieves. He provides some twists and turns to the enjoyment of the crowd, who were not fans of the religious hierarchy.

Jesus tells that a priest and a Levite pass by the poor victim without so much as lifting a hand. The hero in Jesus's story, the one who rescues the man in need, is a commoner from a group who held different beliefs about God.

We're inundated with marketed requests for our money, time, and donated articles. After a while it's tempting to become calloused to these pleas. We're tempted to shut down our philanthropy. In the morning we open the garage door, drive out, go to work, come home, open the garage door, pull in, and close the door behind us, safe and secure. We can go weeks and months without having to interact with our neighbors. But to whom are you a neighbor? To whom do you express responsibility for his or her well-being? Who would think of you when asked to name a friend, a giving person, or a neighborly individual?

A NEIGHBOR IS BEST
DEFINED BY ACTION,
NOT PROXIMITY.

A neighbor is best defined by action, not proximity. Consider your response to the people around you. When paying for merchandise at the checkout stand, ponder how you treat the clerk. The good Samaritan made no excuses. He could have pleaded busyness, lack of medical knowledge, or a religious call for cleanliness as the others had; but he didn't. He used what he had, a donkey, some oil and wine, and a little money. The biggest item he employed was a sensitive heart. In other words, he noticed and responded.

There are people around you, hurting, who've been mugged by life. Use what you have to help them. Offer child-care to a single parent, run an errand for an invalid, drop by to talk to a shut-in, or purchase a surprise for someone who lives close to you. Be the kind of person other people wish they had in their lives. Make the lives of those around you more enjoyable. Cause people to look forward to your visits.

The spheres of your influence are obvious: your immediate neighborhood, work, church, community networks, school and exercise and shopping areas. Neighbors are those who perform kind acts on behalf of others they encounter. Interrupt your schedule. You'll have more places to go and more things to do after you're done with the good deed, but you'll be different because of your obedience. Rush by and you'll arrive at your destination earlier, but there'll be no changed lives in your wake.

LET'S GET PERSONAL

Jesus turns the original question around. He asks, in effect, "Which one was neighborly?" The first question was passive; Jesus's was active. The question is not so much, "Who should I be kind to?" but rather "Are you kind?" Jesus moved the discussion from an analytic, intellectual debate toward a personal, emotional response. "Are you a neighbor?" He was asking the man, . . . and today He asks you.

- How would the people living around you rate you as a neighbor on a 1 to 5 scale? (1 = poor; 5 = great)
- Do you perform random acts of kindness for those around you?
- Who is in your life now that could benefit from your compassion?

It is difficult to find individuals who exude what we all hope for in a neighbor, someone who'll befriend us, taking the time out of their schedules to share a cup of coffee, open a door, carry a package to the car, write a note, or leave a voicemail to say that they were thinking about you.

LET'S GET GOING

1. How do you express your neighborliness?
2. Who has demonstrated neighborly behavior toward you?
3. What can you do this week to model neighborliness?

SESSION

DO YOU STAND OUT?

Now on his way to Jerusalem, Jesus traveled along the border between Samaria and Galilee. As he was going into a village, ten men who had leprosy met him. They stood at a distance and called out in a loud voice, "Jesus, Master, have pity on us!"

When he saw them, he said, "Go, show yourselves to the priests." And as they went, they were cleansed.

One of them, when he saw he was healed, came back, praising God in a loud voice. He threw himself at Jesus' feet and thanked him—and he was a Samaritan.

Jesus asked, "Were not all ten cleansed? Where are the other nine? Was no one found to return and give praise to God except this foreigner?" Then he said to him, "Rise and go; your faith has made you well."

—LUKE 17:11–19

What is it that makes one person stand out from the rest? For some it's a unique physical attribute. For others it's a matter of personal charisma or a dynamic talent. But in today's coaching session, Jesus teaches us about the most consistent means of standing out from the throngs, regardless of looks, personality, or talent. There is nothing so common in society as an ungracious attitude. Whether it's because people are busy and forget, or they assume they're entitled, or they merely underestimate its importance, most fail to adequately express thanks.

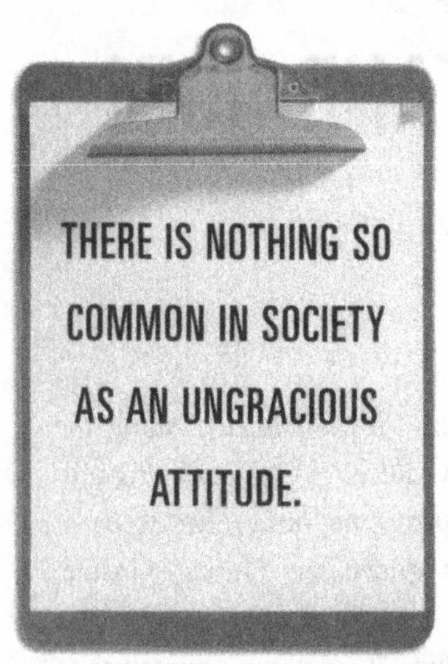
THERE IS NOTHING SO
COMMON IN SOCIETY
AS AN UNGRACIOUS
ATTITUDE.

Jesus was inundated with people who wanted Him for a variety of things. Some yearned for His teachings, others wanted His answers to personal questions, and still others desired healing. When Jesus's travels took Him near a leper colony, ten men came to Him for healing. Civil law did not allow a leper near a nonleper for fear the incurable disease would spread, so they shouted at Him from a distance. Once a leper thought himself to be in remission or healed, he had to go to a priest to receive a clean bill of health before reentering society.

Ten lepers came to Jesus. Ten men left, completely transformed. But only one man returned to say thanks to Jesus. Their healing was no small event. Lepers could not work. They could not live with their families. They could not interact with their friends. They were cut off from society at large. For ten people these negatives went away, yet only one returned to express gratitude. Jesus asked him three questions and then said something quite interesting. He told the man to rise and go, because his faith had made him well. Why did Jesus appear to state the obvious? Perhaps it was merely a summary of the man's situation. Or maybe He was tying the concepts of faith and well-being with the man's expression of appreciation.

Faith is not only a matter of believing in order to get; it is also a matter of believing once you've gotten. Wellness includes both physical and emotional health. Gracious people possess a pleasant and contagious disposition. You've never been offended when someone genuinely told you thanks for a service provided. Conversely, you have felt frustrated when someone failed to acknowledge your service. We all have.

If we surveyed the people who interact with you over the course of any given week, how would they rate your attitude of gratitude on a scale of 1 to 5 (1 = impossible to please; 2 = rarely says thanks; 3 = sometimes expresses gratitude; 4 = usually appreciates others; 5 = very gracious)? Don't limit the list to the obvious people such as your secretary, boss, or coworkers. Consider folks such as your spouse, kids, clients, pastor, your kids' teachers and coaches, the store clerk and waiter, the mailman, housekeeper, gas-station attendant, and bank teller. Every day you have dozens of opportunities to communicate an attitude of gratitude.

Send thank-you notes and e-mails as part of your daily routine. Brainstorm creative ways to say, "I appreciate what you do" to others. Even nice habits can become trite and eventually superficial, so go out of your way to get your point across: THANKS! Consider whom you may be taking for granted. Think of who may feel forgotten.

"Why should I be gracious to people when they're doing what they're paid to do?" Because you're a gracious person and you can't help but exude that spirit. "What if people begin to take it for granted and think I don't have high standards?" The best condition for confronting a wayward employee or a lazy waiter is after you've proven yourself a gracious person, not just an impossible-to-please patron. Being gracious earns you the right to be heard as well as increases the likelihood of being heard well. In the harsh world in which we live, no one is told thanks too often.

Communication involves sending and receiving messages. Regardless of how gracious you think you are, you must hone your skills in conveying your message. Someone said that love is not love until it is given away. Gratitude is not gratitude until it's received. Make sure that the person you are thanking understands what you are doing. Smile. Make eye contact. Use phrases such as, "Thanks for all you do." "I appreciate your hard work." "Thanks for making my life/work better." "I'm sorry for taking you for granted at times." "You do a great job at . . ." "What can I do for you?" Survey those around you to see how you can convey thanks more effectively.

LET'S GET PERSONAL

Jesus's question revealed how impressed He was that this one leper returned (or how unimpressed He was that the others didn't). In today's session Jesus's key question causes us to ponder three more.

- How committed are you to expressing your gratitude?
- To whom do you presently need to extend appreciation?
- What can you do to increase the likelihood that your appreciation is being perceived effectively?

Jesus points out that gracious people stand out from others. That's an encouraging idea when you feel lost in the masses, yearning to make a mark. The added benefit is that people tend to reflect what is modeled for them. The result is that gracious people end up receiving far more grace than those who are ungrateful.

LET'S GET GOING

1. List a dozen people in your life who regularly interact with you in some way.

2. Beside each name write one way you can meaningfully communicate your appreciation.

3. Who in your life unfailingly exudes a gracious attitude? How can you be more like him or her?

SESSION

WHO CARES?

What do you think? If a man owns a hundred sheep, and one of them wanders away, will he not leave the ninety-nine on the hills and go to look for the one that wandered off?
—MATTHEW 18:12

Pastors and priests refer to their calling. Businesspeople and professionals talk about their vocation. The latter term is from the Latin word for "voice, call." In essence, everyone has a call from the Creator related to what God wants that person to do. It's more about making a life than making a living. In today's coaching session we learn about one of these callings. Jesus asks if a man with one hundred sheep would be concerned if one was missing. Would he be satisfied that he had ninety-nine at the end of the day?

The implied response is, "Why of course the shepherd would be concerned about the lost sheep, because he owned one hundred, not ninety-nine." He'd form a search team to go find the lost animal. Sheep sometimes wander from the flock, especially if their grazing leads them over a knoll or if they are spooked by the sight of a wild dog. Shepherds feel responsible for their flock—all of it. They care for their sheep—each one.

Nonshepherds, those who don't really understand the shepherd's heart, are apt to think that this shepherd might have been a little obsessive. "Why couldn't he be satisfied with ninety-nine?" It may have been dark. The evenings are often cold in that part of the world. Convenience would have suggested, "We'll find it later. The sheep will find its way back to the flock. Maybe someone else will come upon it and return it to its owner. Perhaps it was meant to get lost; *c'est la vie*."

Of course Jesus isn't really talking about sheep. That's just a metaphor. Let's say He was talking about your children. What if you have three kids and you go to the mall. When it's time to go home, you can only find two. "Oh well," you say to yourself, "two out of three isn't bad. I still have two. That's better than one or none. Maybe someone else will find him and return him. Maybe he'll find his own way back home. No biggie. I've got other things I can be doing with my time right now." A parent with that attitude would be assigned to social services, faulted for neglect.

Consider whom you need to be reaching for the

Shepherd's sake. God's lost kids are all around us. Part of our purpose for being on earth is to seek them out and return them to the Shepherd. Don't be satisfied with the numbers who have been found. As long as one is lost, the urgency to seek is still there.

You were lost at one time. Someone went after you, whether it was a parent, pastor, friend, neighbor, or family member. Don't believe you were discovered by happenstance. God directed the network that connected you to Him. Realize that you are in your neighborhood, your work, and your circle of influence for a purpose beyond human logic. You are not to be only about your own business. It's also about others.

GOD DIRECTED THE
NETWORK THAT
CONNECTED YOU
TO HIM.

You say, "But I'm just one. There are so many people out there. What can I do?" True, you are just one, and you can't find every one of God's lost kids, but you have been given a mission. Your vocation is to be open to those whom the Shepherd has brought into your pasture. Look for multiple sightings, the connection with the same person in a variety of situations. This person may be your assignment. Observe those who are in your pattern of living, the coffee-shop barista, the grocery clerk, the gas-station attendant, the playground parent, or the gym member who works out at the same time as you, day after day. Seize the opportunity. This may be one of God's lost kids whom you're appointed to find.

Don't just ask about church to find out if a person is lost. Many people escape from God by hiding close to Him, in churches, deceiving others and often themselves. Rather, look in their eyes for a peace that transcends understanding. Listen to their conversations. Look for loving words of others, thoughts of hope, and positive responses regardless of circumstances. These are indicators that they've found their way home. If those signs are not apparent, they may be lost, wandering in the wilderness. Do what you can to earn their trust and lead them to their Shepherd. One of the greatest joys in life is the feeling that comes as you help one of God's lost kids to come home. Don't miss the opportunity. (To learn what it means to be "found," see the appendix on page 183.)

LET'S GET PERSONAL

Jesus certainly cares about animals, but this parable is about His deeper concern—it is about us, His people. Three questions emerge from today's coaching session.

- Who are the lost sheep around you?
- What are the indicators of being lost?

- What are you doing to intentionally connect with these individuals?

Jesus challenges you today to avoid getting so wrapped up in your own little universe that you miss finding God's lost kids around you. You're surrounded by wandering souls every day, some of whom you're destined to reach. You're it. Feel burdened? Good, so does God. He's not satisfied that you and a percentage of others found their way home. He longs for all of His children to come home.

LET'S GET GOING

1. List three potentially lost people around you.

2. What are you doing to reach out to them?

3. How did you find your way back home? (If you're not sure you have, then why not jump to the appendix and read what it means to be found.)

SESSION

26

HOW ARE YOU INVESTING?

"Then another servant came and said, 'Sir, here is your mina; I have kept it laid away in a piece of cloth. I was afraid of you, because you are a hard man. You take out what you did not put in and reap what you did not sow.'

"His master replied, 'I will judge you by your own words, you wicked servant! You knew, did you, that I am a hard man, taking out what I did not put in, and reaping what I did not sow? Why then didn't you put my money on deposit, so that when I came back, I could have collected it with interest?'"

—LUKE 19:20–23

Assumptions are untested ideas that we believe are true. Often they determine how we invest our time, energy, and resources. And we all have them. Most assumptions are adopted unconsciously. We spend little effort investigating what they are, much less whether or not they are reliable. The problem comes when an assumption turns out to be false. We discover that we have been wasting part of our lives. In today's coaching session Jesus provokes us to challenge a commonly held belief.

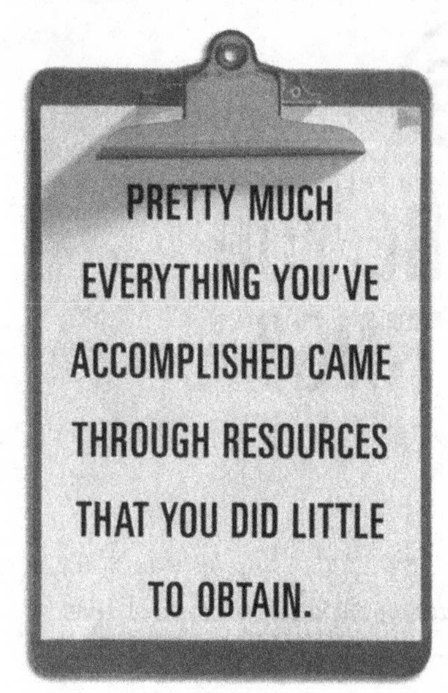
PRETTY MUCH
EVERYTHING YOU'VE
ACCOMPLISHED CAME
THROUGH RESOURCES
THAT YOU DID LITTLE
TO OBTAIN.

The underlying assumption He addresses is that what we have in life is ours, to do with as we please. Whether it's a college degree, a unique talent, or any number of achievements, we presume that these are primarily results of our intelligence and hard work. Although we're tempted to pass blame for failures, we tend to take credit for what we achieve. As perceived owners of these accomplishments we act like masters of our world. We determine where we go, what we do, and whom we pursue. But something is wrong with this assumption. The way that most people pursue success is flawed.

Jesus told a group of His followers a story about a wealthy businessman who entrusted three of his managers with varying amounts of money. One manager took the venture capital, invested it, and returned twice the original amount. The boss commended him and rewarded him appropriately. A second manager was given less, but also doubled the boss's money, winning applause from the owner. Unfortunately, the third manager did little about the capital entrusted to him. When the time came for the profit-loss report, the manager assumed he'd done well by merely preserving the original amount. "Look, I didn't lose your money." The boss came unglued. "You should have at least put it in an interest-bearing account!" The boss fired the manager, calling him "wicked."

The parable is a metaphor for God and those of us in whom He's invested gifts, talents, relationships, opportunities, IQ, personality, and experiences. When you think about it, pretty much everything you've accomplished came through resources that you did little to obtain. Studies show that your IQ is mostly established at birth. Many opportunities in Western civilization were afforded because you "happened" to be born in a free-enterprise system. Your basic temperament, metabolism, physique, and early-life influences were given to you from others.

Jesus encourages us to consider the possibility that we don't own anything, that we're temporary caretakers for an Owner/Boss. You weren't born with any costly possessions, and you won't leave this earth with any tangible asset. You're basically a renter, lessee, tenant—regardless of the wording that banks and lawyers use to describe the relationship you have with "stuff." We're pioneers versus settlers; transients versus homeowners. We're not really citizens on earth; we're foreigners, passing through. We cling to our gifts and achievements as though they were ours. We are really managers who have been entrusted to use what we have been given for optimum benefits, not for our honor and pleasure, but for the Boss's. A good employee always considers what the owner wants for his business.

LET'S GET PERSONAL

Do you think Jesus is striving to become your financial advisor, or does He have a bigger agenda? Jesus challenges you to reconsider some of your basic assumptions about why you're here and what it is you're to be doing with what you've got.

- How would your daily life change if you believed that you were a steward of God's gifts and opportunities instead of the sole proprietor?
- What would you do differently if you knew you'd have to give an account for your choice of words, use of time, development of relationships, and deployment of talents?
- Would you spend all your money on yourself, or do you think God might have you invest some of it in those who have less or with agencies whose mission statements involves benefiting people?

When you live for yourself, you're missing an important tenet of faith. While you must take care of the basic needs of your family, keeping your assets and achievements to yourself is an unwise plan. God expects a return. You're not here to do what you please. Take your time, talent, and treasure seriously . . . because it really belongs to Someone else. In the big picture of life you're called to a higher purpose than your own plans. It's not about you. Life is bigger than most of us assume.

Managing God's assets well has benefits for you. Rewards come from the wise use of your resources. Realizing you don't ultimately carry the burden that comes with ownership is a huge relief. You're not the source of all that exists or is to be. You have avenues of acquiring wisdom, support, and resources that transcend your own limited universe. So long as you're a diligent steward of what's been temporarily entrusted to you, you can sleep well at night. It's when we believe ourselves to be our own gods, owning all we possess, that we develop ulcers and heart disease and feel the need to self-medicate. Jesus is helping you enjoy the fruit of your labor by taking the burden of ownership from your shoulders.

LET'S GET GOING

1. What are your basic assumptions about ownership in life? Have you formed these ideas without seriously considering their reliability?

2. If you lived as an entrusted manager of talent, relationships, and opportunities, how might this attitude change the way you deal with work, family, friendships, time, and money?

3. What possible benefits could result from living as if God is the Boss and Owner of all you have?

SESSION

27

WHAT MAKES A GOOD LEADER?

Jesus said to them, "The kings of the Gentiles lord it over them; and those who exercise authority over them call themselves Benefactors. But you are not to be like that. Instead, the greatest among you should be like the youngest, and the one who rules like the one who serves. For who is greater, the one who is at the table or the one who serves? Is it not the one who is at the table? But I am among you as one who serves."

—LUKE 22:25–27

The purpose of leadership is to facilitate groups of people to accomplish more together than they could as individuals. Leaders are people who help catalyze more leadership. The true influence of leadership actually lies within those who are led. If people decide not to follow, then a person ceases to be a leader. Many people aspire to be leaders—for the wrong reasons. They yearn for power, pay, notoriety, and an assortment of perceived perks for being the go-to person. But in today's coaching session, Jesus turns the tables on the way many view leaders and positions of authority.

Jesus notes that certain leaders lord influence over others. They flaunt it; they get a kick out of using it; they build their egos by extending their influence. He says they "call themselves Benefactors." Healthy leading serves others. A true leader is not one who calls himself a benefactor, but whom others refer to as a benefactor.

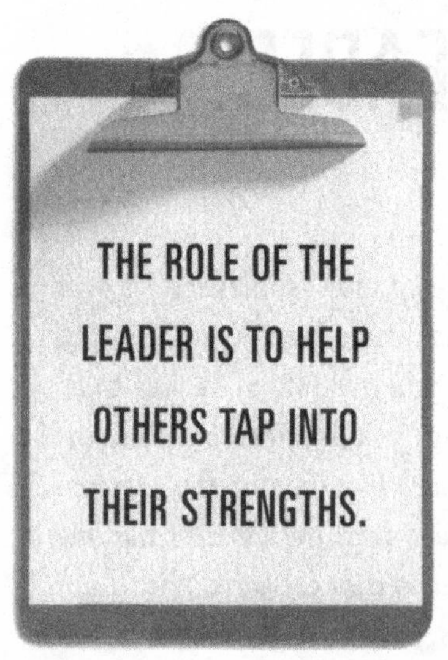
THE ROLE OF THE
LEADER IS TO HELP
OTHERS TAP INTO
THEIR STRENGTHS.

If you are a leader, think about the kind of service you provide. While a good leader is not above doing the work of others, strong leadership empowers others to do their own work. The role of the leader is to help others tap into their strengths. Through organizing, vision casting, problem solving, and resource gathering, leaders serve by helping others serve.

The attitude of a Jesus-style leader is that of a servant. Jesus challenges us to rethink the way we go about leading. Servant leaders see themselves as servants more than leaders. Some servants use a washcloth and a pail of water to serve. Others use power tools, computers, cooking utensils, and sales skills to serve. Leaders are merely servants who use their ability to influence others to work together.

One benefit of servant leading is that it requires far less maintenance. When you lord your influence, you're always on the prowl to make sure others don't circumvent your authority. You're concerned with how you're doing for ego reasons, instead of genuine concern for others. You base your value on how successful you are. The inner battle for meaning and purpose rages because there's always one more thing to conquer. Finding fulfillment in helping others accomplish their appointed tasks will seem insufficient when you lead for reasons other than to serve.

Jesus says that the *greatest* should be like the *youngest*. He didn't say they actually were the youngest, the least experienced, or the most naive. He said leaders should have their attitude. When you claim to have all the answers, brag about your title or position, or use your power for personal reasons, your leadership potential is reduced. Don't let your role change *who* you are. The best leaders have servant hearts.

Servanthood should not be confused with weakness. People may need to be confronted, dismissed, or challenged. Difficult decisions need to be made. A servant leader strives to think of the larger organization while valuing the individual. This precarious balance perpetuates organizational health, but not at the sacrifice of human dignity. The guiding light is always appropriateness. Leaders who lord over others generally have one way, their way. Servant leading is often more difficult because it requires self-restraint, relational savvy, and patience.

Servant leaders are humble, and they resist pulling rank in order to make a difficult decision. True servant leaders do not manipulate with words and threaten with authority. They persuade through team building and motivate with encouragement. Servant leaders are not wimps, but at times they have to deal with the accusations of being too soft.

Behind the scenes you see how the true leaders are building people, not just organizations. They are listening, thinking, and applying themselves. They're getting things done. People are inspired to follow them and want to be on their team, because together they accomplish greater feats in a more enjoyable way. They experience success as well as community.

LET'S GET PERSONAL

Today's coaching session prompts us to do some soul searching about how we influence others.

- Who do you identify with as a leader, and what traits do you want to emulate?
- What kind of leader do you want to be?
- What are you doing to pursue a servant-leader attitude?

Servant leading doesn't start in the corporate office, government, school system, or worship community. It begins in the heart. You must decide for yourself what kind of influence you will be. You can govern by fear and intimidation, or you can pick a new paradigm and lead with intelligence, act with humility, and build through relationships. Greatness is not in how many serve you, but in how many you serve.

LET'S GET GOING

1. Do you know anyone who is a servant leader? How does this person influence others without a heavy hand?

2. Do you know anyone who is a nonservant leader? How does this person influence without a servant's attitude?

3. List three benefits of servant leading that outweigh the world's prescription for effective leadership.

SESSION

28

WHAT ARE YOU SLEEPING THROUGH?

He came back and found [the disciples] sound asleep. He said to Peter, "Simon, you went to sleep on me? Can't you stick it out with me a single hour?"

—MARK 14:37 MSG

There's a time to sleep and a time to be alert. When we confuse those times, we lose golden opportunities and put ourselves at risk. Today Jesus teaches us about staying alert and taking action when the time is right. To Jesus's disciples the events and late hour of this specific evening tempted them to let down their guards, even though Jesus had told them how overwhelmed with sorrow He was and had asked them to watch while He prayed. They may have been wearied by the week's events or merely feeling relaxed following the Passover wine and food. But their eyes were heavy, the sun was gone, and darkness coaxed them to slumber. Seemingly oblivious to the heavy heart of their leader, one by one they drifted off.

But this night was important. Jesus knew that He was about to be captured, put on mock trial, and crucified. He had already predicted that Peter would betray Him. Peter needed to be praying for strength, not snoozing from exhaustion. But what could Jesus do? The others didn't "get it." They were sleeping on duty. He could not continue waking them up, because he needed to pray.

Something in your life is begging for your attention. Being attentive to it is important. In today's session, sleeping can also be seen as a metaphor for procrastination, denial, or irresponsibility.

One day a farmer stood with his son in a bean field and pointed to a lone corn stalk growing above the bean plants. "What's that?" he asked.

The boy looked at his father inquisitively, wondering why his father had asked him such a simple question.

"That's a corn stalk," the boy said.

"No, it's a weed," the father responded.

The boy thought to himself, *No, it's not. We have acres of cornfields on our farm. Dad knows the difference.* But he responded again. "That's a corn stalk."

The father said, "No, a corn stalk in a bean field is a weed because it doesn't belong there."

Perhaps you're avoiding something difficult. You may be doing something else in its place. Plowing through difficult situations is painful. The "wall" is an emotional and physical barrier that long-distance runners face when the body's chemistry runs low on epinephrine, our natural painkiller. Working through a marital dispute, staying up late to finish a work project, rehearsing an important presentation one more time, enduring a workout at the gym, or pushing through times of needed prayer are examples of when self-discipline must dominate. We're tempted to sleep, watch TV, walk away, or do something more fun. Sometimes the monotony of a task makes it seem unbearable. But succumbing to our emotions and physical yearnings means defeat. If we fail to fight through the fatigue, the pain of enduring, and momentary temptation to check out, we'll be shirking our duty.

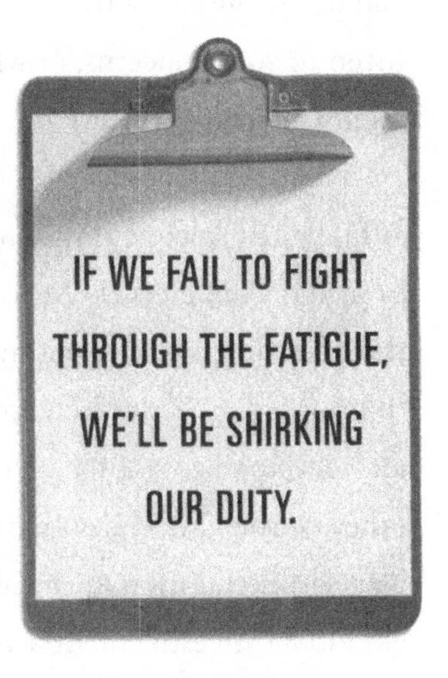
IF WE FAIL TO FIGHT
THROUGH THE FATIGUE,
WE'LL BE SHIRKING
OUR DUTY.

You may need a good support system. Having someone to call in the middle of the night to mop up water from a broken water heater is a good thing. Knowing who'd stay up late with you if you needed someone to work through a personal matter is invaluable. When you have a friend who knows you well enough to read between the lines when you're heartbroken and in need of support, it is worth more than gold. Jesus had invested three years with a small group of men who did not perceive the heaviness in His life on this fateful night. Blessed is the person who has even one or two friends close enough to call in the middle of the night, who'll pray with you, who will listen to your concerns, or who will just sit with you during a family member's operation.

People commonly say, "Call me if you need anything." While often sincere, this statement can also be a quick release from immediate effort. Most people will never follow up on the offer, unless you've put in the time and energy beforehand to prove yourself sincerely interested in helping. Most people are too proud to ask for help or just reluctant to burden another person. They may find it easier to give help than to receive it; certainly than to ask for it. Maintaining sufficient emotional investment in a person close to you will increase the chance of being asked for help. Since most of us like to think of ourselves as self-sufficient, one of the greatest compliments is for a friend to request a hand when it is truly needed.

LET'S GET PERSONAL

Jesus was not whining to His friend. He was calling His disciple to a better place. Jesus's coaching session causes us to consider three things.

- What should you be doing today?
- Who can you count on to "stay awake" with you when you're in a crisis?
- To whom are you this kind of friend?

Jesus teaches us so much with His question. He calls us to be a friend, and He frees us to admit that we need one. Jesus knew His disciples needed sleep; they were human. But to be sleeping when you should be alert to the needs of others is wrong. Understanding both timing and priorities is an invaluable lesson about making life work.

LET'S GET GOING

1. What opportunity are you sleeping through? Who is in your life to awaken you?
2. Why are you avoiding this priority in your life?
3. What are the potential risks of procrastinating—doing something else instead of what is most important?

SESSION

WHO PULLS YOUR STRINGS?

On the third day a wedding took place at Cana in Galilee. Jesus' mother was there, and Jesus and his disciples had also been invited to the wedding. When the wine was gone, Jesus' mother said to him, "They have no more wine."

"Dear woman, why do you involve me?" Jesus replied, "My time has not yet come."

—JOHN 2:1–4

While Jesus claimed that His primary purpose was to serve instead of to be served, He seems to throw us for a loop in today's coaching session. During a wedding event the hosts ran out of wine. Knowing Jesus's ability to do miracles and perhaps in order to make Him go public with His gifts, Jesus's mother prompts Him to respond to the situation. Jesus resists by asking her a question.

We've all been in situations where someone close to us asked us to do something that we did not feel comfortable about. When this happens the temptation is to comply for the sake of the person asking. But just as others have a right to walk across relational bridges to make their requests, we sometimes need to activate our right to decline them.

Ironically, after Jesus refuses His mother's request to "fix the problem," He does the thing she asks. Did He feel badly about asking her to mind her own business? A more reasonable conclusion is that sometimes we need to establish the right motive for doing something. To turn water into wine at the wedding because the situation called for it is one thing; to do so in order to please a person or show off is another. We learn an invaluable lesson here, not about selfishness, but about healthy motives. We should comply with a person's request when it is right. The same request by the same person in a different setting may deserve an opposite response.

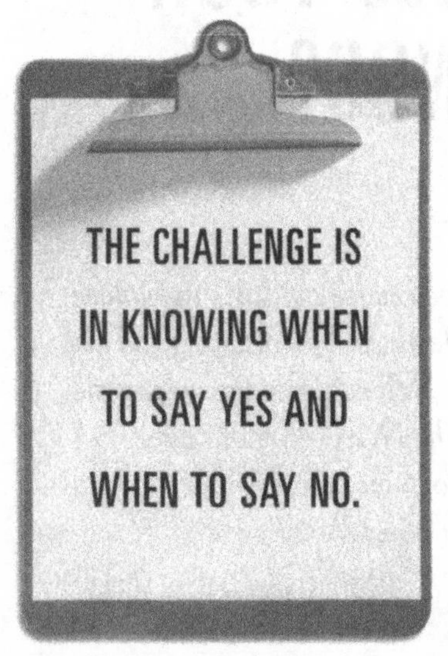
THE CHALLENGE IS
IN KNOWING WHEN
TO SAY YES AND
WHEN TO SAY NO.

A strong person is not someone who always says no. Nor is a strong person one who always says yes. The challenge is in knowing when to say yes and when to say no. Knowing when you should comply with a person's request and when you need to decline takes wisdom. If you say yes when you should say no, you will not be fair to yourself or others. You'll feel manipulated, used, and resentful. When you sense that you're always at the disposal of others, your self-esteem will diminish. As a result, you'll be less effective in your relationships. You'll also be unavailable to respond to more important matters because you'll be preoccupied with lesser ones.

As a result, of rarely or never saying no, people feel overloaded and erect unnecessary barriers in their relationships. They avoid getting close to people for fear of being used. This emotional separation is often unintentional, but it results in loneliness. The distant person is often one who previously failed to establish healthy boundaries.

People pleasers do a disservice to others by responding to whims of "string pullers." Healthy and unhealthy service may look alike on the outside, but one is positive and the other is poison. Because motives are difficult to ascertain, it is impossible for us to confidently know why another person is asking us to respond to their desires. A person needs wisdom to understand the motive of the person who is asking and why.

We all have people in our lives who try to manipulate us, but even non-string-pullers can make inappropriate requests. A boss, child, sibling, close friend, boyfriend or girlfriend, spouse, client, or stranger can ask us to do things that we should graciously decline. Establishing exit lines beforehand is sometimes helpful. "I'd love to do it at another time." "This wouldn't be the right thing for me." "Thanks for asking, but I need to say no." "It would be good if you can find someone else to do this for you." "I appreciate your thinking of me, but you'll need to do this on your own this time." "I need to stick to my decision." "I appreciate your respecting my choice in this situation." A variety of respectful answers can be rehearsed if you find yourself stalling under pressure. If nothing else, you can put off the decision until you're able to think through a response, but it is important to follow through with a no, not just procrastinate and hope it will go away.

LET'S GET PERSONAL

Jesus's question was not a means of avoidance. His question models an appropriate way to decline what one is not called to do. Today's coaching session helps us realize that there are times when we need to decline requests by others even if they do not understand.

- What are you doing to please people instead of doing what you are called to do?
- Who are the string-pullers in your life?
- How can you confront these string-pullers in a way that will preserve respect for you without offending the other person?

People will try to influence us at times to do things we should resist. Do not fault them for this, but don't relent in saying no. Doing the right thing with the right motives empowers you to better serve them later—without compromising your standards. Walk away without guilt. Sometimes you need to stand up, talk back, confront, and avoid being a doormat. This is not about serving less, but serving better and appropriately.

LET'S GET GOING

1. Think of a current request on your life. What is the risk in not responding to the other person in the way he or she wants?
2. What are the risks of not resisting, of giving in to the person's request?
3. Write a response that preserves their feelings and protects your free will.

SESSION

DO YOU WANT TO GET WELL?

A great number of disabled people used to lie [beside a pool called Bethesda]—the blind, the lame, the paralyzed. One who was there had been an invalid for thirty-eight years. When Jesus saw him lying there and learned that he had been in this condition for a long time, he asked him, "Do you want to get well?"

—JOHN 5:3–6

The person who has discovered his or her purpose in life realizes that ultimately it is to serve others. You may serve them as a retail clerk, janitor, CEO, middle manager, schoolteacher, pastor, homemaker, or personal trainer. Regardless of the role or tools, your Creator has called you to be of benefit to others. Even though this is true, when others come to you for assistance, sometimes you need to resist their request. You need to respond wisely, which means discerning whether or not they really want help or if they truly desire to get better.

One day Jesus happened upon a large group of disabled people, more than likely gathered to beg for money and in hopes of being healed. Jesus went to one man specifically. We don't know if He healed everyone. But Jesus asked this man a strange question, "Do you want to get well?" If the man had been an invalid for nearly forty years and was obviously with other disabled folks beside a place of healing, why would Jesus insensitively ask the question, "Do you want to be healed?" Who wouldn't want to be healed? What was He thinking?

When people complain about a problem they have—a relationship gone sideways, a job falling apart, or difficult circumstances—sometimes you do well to ask the question, "Do you want it to get better?" Wouldn't everyone want to be cured? The reasons are complex, but the truth is that they often do not.

Sometimes people don't want to get well because it would remove their reasons for complaining. Many people like to gripe because of a damaged self-image or a warped habit of focusing on the negative. They act like they want circumstances to get better, but they really don't. If things got better, what would they have to complain about?

By getting well, the man would have had to go back to work, leave his longtime disabled friends, give up familiar surroundings, and return to the mainstream of society.

Significant change would be required. Even disabilities can become comfort zones. Some people would rather die than change. So they cling to their problems. The infirmity becomes a security blanket, a socially acceptable means of avoiding responsibilities.

Sometimes we hold on to our disabilities because labeling ourselves is easier than changing. "I'm disabled." This can become a license for me to sit and do nothing, to complain about life, or to induce others to pity me and serve me. While these statements seem quite harsh, the morbid truth is that all of us are tempted to hide behind our inadequacies at times because it's easier than getting better. "I'm a middle child." "I'm from a dysfunctional family." "I'm Irish." "I'm a redhead." "I'm an only child." "I had it rough growing up." "I'm an alcoholic." "I'm ADHD." The excuses people give for their lack of compassion and responsibility are legion. Some excuses are valid, but we still need to ask, "Do you want to get well? Do you want to get beyond your disability, even if you can't get rid of it?"

SOMETIMES WE HOLD
ON TO OUR DISABILITIES
BECAUSE LABELING
OURSELVES IS EASIER
THAN CHANGING.

Jesus teaches us that we can't assume people want help

when they complain about something. Just because they come to church, they're not necessarily interested in finding God. Just because they stay married, they're not necessarily looking for a loving, committed relationship. Just because they join a team doesn't mean they want to win. Sometimes we embrace our disabilities as a way to hide from growth. We want a payday without the workweek. We desire the reward without the risk. We look for the trophy without expending the effort.

We often don't ask this question of others because it is counterintuitive to wonder if a person wants our help. But the benefits of inquiring are significant. By asking the question up front we can avoid investing countless hours of effort, which will end in frustration. The confrontation, when appropriate, can also help the afflicted person come to terms with his or her motivations and responsibilities.

LET'S GET PERSONAL

Jesus's question was not for His own sake, but for the sake of the man, He asked. Jesus is asking you to consider three things.

- How have you been using your challenges to avoid responsibility for your actions and responses to others?
- Have you become comfortable with discomfort?
- Is there a possibility that you're looking for an excuse to be depressed or to fail?

If your challenges went away, you'd be expected to achieve, to succeed, to serve, or to be more loving. While it's easier to see the potential avoidance of others, our healing starts by honestly looking in the mirror.

The inward application of this coaching session is that Jesus calls you to consider your disabilities. Perhaps it is your current situation, a divorce, a bad job dismissal, a less than desirable marriage, or any number of conditions. We're quick to complain, but do we want to get well?

LET'S GET GOING

1. Who are people in your life who love to complain and act like they want help, but probably don't want to improve their situations?
2. Why is it important to determine whether or not people actually want your help?
3. What labels or past experiences are you dragging into the future, perhaps as excuses to hide behind, which may be preventing you from growing?

SESSION

IS YOUR LOVE FOR REAL?

When they had finished eating, Jesus said to Simon Peter, "Simon son of John, do you truly love me more than these?"

"Yes, Lord," he said, "you know that I love you."

Jesus said, "Feed my lambs."

Again Jesus said, "Simon son of John, do you truly love me?"

He answered, "Yes, Lord, you know that I love you."

Jesus said, "Take care of my sheep."

The third time he said to him, "Simon son of John, do you love me?"

Peter was hurt because Jesus asked him the third time, "Do you love me?" He said, "Lord, you know all things; you know that I love you."

—JOHN 21:15–17

Imagine how disconcerting it must have been to be Peter, surrounded by his peers, to hear Jesus ask him three times if he loved Him. He could understand once, for by this time the others probably knew that he'd publicly denied knowing his Master three times. But Jesus asked again and again. What was He getting at? Why did He repeat Himself? Did He not believe Peter's first and second answers? What was He looking for from Peter?

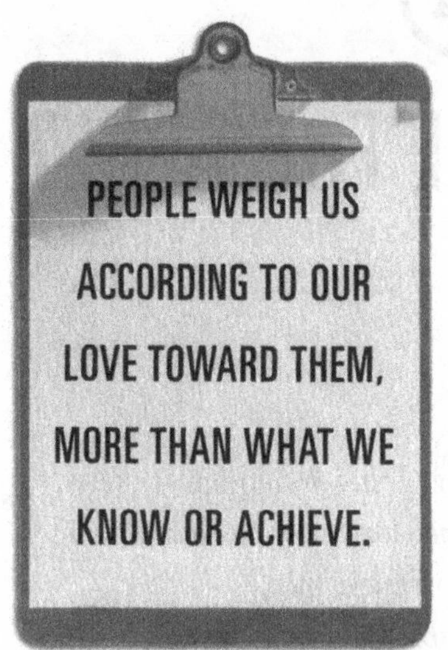
PEOPLE WEIGH US
ACCORDING TO OUR
LOVE TOWARD THEM,
MORE THAN WHAT WE
KNOW OR ACHIEVE.

Undoubtedly embarrassed and put on the spot, Peter must have sensed that a point was being made, but what? Nowhere in Jesus's words do we find condemnation or even a mention of the previous denials. Jesus was teaching something new in this lesson. While Peter had previously mouthed allegiance, the problem was that his words lacked action.

Today's coaching session asks, "Is your love for real?" If we accomplish great feats, make lots of money, govern large groups of people, but aren't loving in the process, we'll have achieved little—or at least nothing worth writing home about (see 1 Corinthians 13). Boil life down to its most basic components, and you'll find love in the residue. People weigh us according to our love toward them, more than what we know or achieve. It's a subtle but powerful truth.

Solving the puzzle begins by defining the term *love*. Some say that love can't be defined. You recognize it when you see it. Others suggest that you can't explain it, but you know when it's missing. Jesus was not referring to a romantic or sensual passion between a husband and wife. Nor was He describing a fondness for a pet or hobby, or a fizzy emotion that percolates in teenage coeds. Jesus was using a unique term that He popularized in His teachings, referring to a supreme brand of love, not based on emotion. It is sometimes defined as love without strings. It is choosing to treat another person with value, in spite of how he or she treats you.

Jesus likely asked Peter three times because He could tell that Peter didn't understand. Communicators use repetition to make sure hearers comprehend the message. While the English language does not pick this up, Peter actually doesn't use the same word for *love* that Jesus did. Peter uses a word that referred to friendship in his day, an emotional sort of "buddy" love. Jesus repeated Himself to make a point. Talk is cheap. Love is an act of will, a decision displayed in action.

Jesus's question for us today will require some concentrated effort. The question asked, "Do you love Me?" is followed by the declaration, "then feed My sheep." Authentic love always results in some sort of action, a tangible expression. You can give without loving, but you can't love without giving. If someone monitored your life for a week, watching the way you invested your time and spent your money, think about what they'd say you love. People need to recognize a person's love before it is accepted as such.

Most of the time people assume others sense their love more than they actually do. A better judge of the quality of love is looking for benchmarks, a means of measuring love in tangible ways. If we hide behind the idea of love as merely an internal feeling, no one can accuse us of being unloving . . . or hold us accountable. If you went on trial to defend your love for your family, friends, or your God, consider the evidence you'd produce.

Caring for Jesus's followers (feed My sheep) was important to Him. Therefore, it became an indicator of whether or not Peter understood Jesus's interests and, as a result, whether or not Peter would respond. Sometimes our gestures of love to others do not resonate with what they value and therefore fail to be recognized as love. We tend to love people according to our preferences, not theirs. Unless you know a person's love language, it will be difficult to communicate love effectively.

Consider the ways in which others love you. Sometimes we discount demonstrations of love or fail to let them register in our hearts. We overlook tangible expressions that others make and fail to appreciate and thank them. Look for actions of others that convey love.

From this coaching lesson we learn three things:

1. The best kind of love transcends emotion and conditions; it's a decision.

2. Authentic love results in tangible expression, not just an inner feeling.

3. Love requires that we understand what is important to another person.

LET'S GET PERSONAL

Jesus certainly heard Peter's answer to His question the first and second times. And He must also have been aware of the sincerity of Peter's answer. However, Jesus also knew what Peter needed to learn. His coaching session today has three prompts:

- How do you measure your love for others?

- How can you tell when people authentically love and esteem you?

- What do you need to do to communicate your love more effectively?

Establishing your love for others and their love for you is a healthy process toward growth and maturity, even if assessing it creates some tension. The goal is to become more loving, which is the ultimate expression of growth and maturity.

SESSION 31

LET'S GET GOING

1. To whom in your life do you demonstrate love?

2. Who in your life demonstrates love to you?

3. How can you improve the effectiveness of your love?

AFTERWORD

Many people consider Jesus primarily to be a renowned leader and teacher. To others He was a gifted prophet, a divine messenger. Still others consider Him to be God incarnate, a member of the Trinity who created the world as we know it and who continues to reside in those who put their faith in Him. Free will allows us to believe any or none of these opinions about Jesus. I am open to discussing my personal acceptance of orthodox Christianity, which acknowledges the divinity of Christ and His desire for us to know and follow Him personally, intimately. Feel free to contact me via my Web site at www.leadingideas.org for further information.

Regardless of your personal beliefs, the questions that Jesus asked as part of His teachings provoke even the sagest among us to consider how we can become better. I hope you enjoyed these coaching sessions that target the most essential principles of life. In closing, may I offer this prayer for you to use to advance your development?

God, thank You for sending Jesus, who taught us so many

things that have to do with life, love, and the pursuit of what is important. Please guide my fellow pilgrims as they leave this book and progress on life's road. Let them experience new insights, deeper faith, broader love, and richer opportunities as they mature. Introduce them to writers, teachers, leaders, and mentors who will guide them further in Your ways. I thank You for moments we've had to share through this simple book. Amen *(Let it be).*

APPENDIX

WHAT WE MEAN BY BEING "FOUND"

(FROM SESSION 25)

Jesus talked quite a bit about "lost things" (see Luke 15:4–7; 8–10; 11–32). He even said that His purpose was to seek and save the "lost" (see Luke 19:10). Good people get lost. Bad people get lost. It's not necessarily that anyone is trying to be lost. They're just not sure how to find what they're looking for—like a visitor to a city, driving around without a map. We're all newcomers to life. We've not been here before, and so even the smartest, most talented, and most sincere among us needs directions.

The simple picture of Christianity is that as spiritual beings, souls with bodies, we're on a spiritual trek that got interrupted by a core of self-centeredness, much like a bad computer virus. Everyone wrestles with this orientation. No one is born without this deviant gene in his or her DNA (see Romans 3:23). It is this self-centered bent that fights our desire to let God lead us. The word *repent* literally means to have a "change of mind." Therefore, when you repent, you turn from a life bent on doing what you want toward a life of doing what God wants. While it seems as if you're giving up, you're really just changing mind-sets (see Romans 8:5–8)—buying into a new belief system.

If we acknowledge and confess this orientation to follow ourselves rather than God, then He's willing to forgive us and give us another chance (see 1 John 1:9). When you accept this new orientation in life, transferring leadership to Jesus, He accepts you into His family (see John 1:12). That's what it means to be *found*, to end your *lostness*.

My perspective is that Jesus is more than just a noble teacher and wise philosopher. I believe, by faith versus scientific proof, that Jesus is the Son of God and that He came not only to teach, but to live and die for us. While you don't need to believe this to enjoy this book and learn from the teachings of Jesus, it is my belief that the content in the book will make more sense if you admit your *lostness* and humbly commit to letting the Spirit of Jesus lead you in your daily life, work, relationships, and worship. If you do not feel ready to make that decision, then ponder it for a while. Don't put it on the shelf or ignore it until you've thoroughly investigated the teachings of Jesus and considered the possibilities of having Him in your life. Granted, the stakes are high, but the potential payoff is out of this world.

9 781451 623789